SpringerBriefs in Ge

More information about this series at http://www.springer.com/series/10050

Kristof Van Assche · Petruţa Teampău

Local Cosmopolitanism

Imagining and (Re-)Making Privileged Places

Kristof Van Assche
Faculty of Extension
University of Alberta
Edmonton, AB
Canada

Petruța Teampău
Faculty of Political, Administrative
  and Communication Sciences
Babes Bolyai University
Cluj-Napoca
Romania

ISSN 2211-4165　　　　　　　ISSN 2211-4173　(electronic)
SpringerBriefs in Geography
ISBN 978-3-319-19029-7　　　ISBN 978-3-319-19030-3　(eBook)
DOI 10.1007/978-3-319-19030-3

Library of Congress Control Number: 2015939162

Springer Cham Heidelberg New York Dordrecht London
© The Author(s) 2015
This work is subject to copyright. All rights are reserved by the Publisher, whether the whole or part of the material is concerned, specifically the rights of translation, reprinting, reuse of illustrations, recitation, broadcasting, reproduction on microfilms or in any other physical way, and transmission or information storage and retrieval, electronic adaptation, computer software, or by similar or dissimilar methodology now known or hereafter developed.
The use of general descriptive names, registered names, trademarks, service marks, etc. in this publication does not imply, even in the absence of a specific statement, that such names are exempt from the relevant protective laws and regulations and therefore free for general use.
The publisher, the authors and the editors are safe to assume that the advice and information in this book are believed to be true and accurate at the date of publication. Neither the publisher nor the authors or the editors give a warranty, express or implied, with respect to the material contained herein or for any errors or omissions that may have been made.

Printed on acid-free paper

Springer International Publishing AG Switzerland is part of Springer Science+Business Media (www.springer.com)

Contents

Part I Introduction and Basic Concepts

1 Back to Basics: Cosmopolitanism? 3
    References 6

Part II A Broader Angle

2 A Brief Orientation in the Literature 9
    References 12

3 Cosmopolitanism in the Light of Philosophical Tradition 15
    References 23

4 Cosmopolitanism and Networks: Odessa, Trieste, Tbilisi 25
    4.1 Trieste 29
    4.2 Odessa 33
    4.3 Tbilisi 38
    4.4 Narratives and Networks and These Three 41
    References 44

Part III The Small Worlds of Cosmopolitanism: Sulina

5 Introduction: Sulina as Center and Margin 49
    References 55

v

6 Narratives of Place and Self... 57
  6.1 Autobiography, Biography, and Place 57
  6.2 Gatekeepers and Promoters of Memory...................... 68
  6.3 A History of Marginality 76
  6.4 New Borders and Boundaries................................ 81
  References... 84

7 Identities on the Move.. 87
  7.1 Fluid Identities and Migration 87
  7.2 Performance of Multiculturalism and Urban Space............ 93
  7.3 Vanished Groups and Their Narrative Impact 96
  7.4 Vanished Places and Their Narrative Impact 98
  References... 101

8 Narratives, Networks and Policies (Sulina and Beyond)............ 103
  8.1 Changing Landscapes and Reconstruction of Identity............ 103
  8.2 Past, Future and Policy.................................... 110
  References... 113

Part IV Small and Large

9 Local Cosmopolitanism and Governance 117
  9.1 Introduction: Local Cosmopolitanism Revisited 117
  9.2 The Real... 119
  9.3 Trieste and the Others..................................... 122
  9.4 Towards a Governance Frame 124
  9.5 Policies and Steering 127
  References... 130

Part I
Introduction and Basic Concepts

Chapter 1
Back to Basics: Cosmopolitanism?

Abstract In this chapter we outline the basic assumptions and concepts structuring the book, clarifying that cosmopolitanism for us is necessarily a local construct, making sense of circulating narratives at other scales, linking with larger networks, and reinterpreting self, past, present and future in a manner that allows for a persuasive narrative of pre-figuration or eminent representation of what will be eminent globally. We emphasize that our theory has to address narratives and networks in multi-level governance, that it has to understand that only what can be interpreted, coordinated, acted upon locally can materialize, and that the theory has to discern the various functions of cosmopolitan narratives in a community.

Keywords Cosmopolitanism · Narrative · Network · Contingency · Localism · Privilege · Ethics

What is cosmopolitanism? Different times, places and theories offer different answers. Is it good or bad? Can we render a place cosmopolitan? A person? How? To these questions we find a similar variety of answers. Another recurring question: does cosmopolitanism have a normative dimension at all, in other words, is it something either to strive for or to avoid? A separate set of questions pertains to the genesis and history of cosmopolitanism: does it even have a history? Is it changing? Is there still a need to speak of cosmopolitanism in a globalizing world?

We feel there is still a need to talk about cosmopolitanism. Because the talk of globalization has produced a profound confusion regarding the history of globalization, the previously existing forms of cooperation, coordination, diffusion and exchange. Because cities portray themselves as the sole bearers of a positively presented form of cosmopolitanism, because cities and regions compete and market themselves as ahead of the curve by being more like the rest, a better reflection of the most modern version of modernity. Because post-modern thinkers often forgot the recurring mechanisms in local constructions of self, place and history.

In this book, we focus on places and communities associating with cosmopolitan ideals, not on persons and not on negative interpretations of cosmopolitanism.

We start from the idea that cosmopolitanism always involves *an image of the whole in the part*, that means, an image of a larger world in a community belonging to that world. This implies a whole and a part, and a relation between those two. Parts make up the whole and the whole shapes the parts. It implies an image: the part cannot be the whole, and cannot know the whole exhaustively. There is always selection and *interpretation*. There are relations between parts and whole that are not grasped by the interpretations of these relations: what is seen locally as the presence or absence of cosmopolitanism per definition differs from the actual set of relations between parts and whole (cf. Luhmann 1990). We will further explain and expand on this starting point later on in the book.

Cosmopolitan ideals, in legal and political terms, and cosmopolitan narratives, on what are cosmopolitan places and behaviors, are and have always been *constructed and reconstructed locally*, and had many different functions in local communities with cosmopolitan aspirations or memories. At the same time, these narrative forms and functions are not constructed in imaginary freedom in those communities: competing narratives and the forces associated with shifting political, economic and cultural networks make it more or less likely that these narratives arise, acquire local functions, and might be spread elsewhere (Delanty 2009).

Cosmopolitanism is thus a matter of changing images of the whole in the part, of changing functions of those images locally, and of actually changing relations between parts and whole. For that reason, we speak of *local cosmopolitanism*, meaning that every cosmopolitanism is local, and co-evolving with both local and global scales. We will point out that the narratives of the global and a relation with can sometimes be largely a product of local shifts, in other cases a local response to larger changes, to direct competition in a similar global structure, or changes in that structure. Local cosmopolitanism can in other words be a response to many things, and it can serve many purposes. We will argue that an understanding of local cosmopolitanism as part and parcel of evolving governance renders it more easy to grasp shifts between localism and cosmopolitanism, distinctions between versions of cosmopolitanism, and the balance between remembering and forgetting of certain relations with larger wholes. Understanding it in the context of governance opens up new avenues to think of local responses and contributions to globalization, and to discern options for policy and planning to productively deal with the local/global dialectics and with competing variants of cosmopolitanism (Van Assche et al. 2014). Cosmopolitan realities and mythologies can both have positive functions in a community, and de-mystification cannot be the final result of the analysis.

We intend to unpack our topic by first looking at the current literature and then the underlying and grounding philosophical traditions of cosmopolitanism, then by means of a brief comparison of three cities with aspects of cosmopolitan histories: Trieste, Odessa and Tbilisi. Trieste, on the Adriatic coast, was a center of Habsburg trade for centuries, de facto the only large port in the empire, and for a long time its third city. Odessa, on the Black Sea coast, was founded much later, in the late 18th century, after the final conquest of Southern Ukraine on the Crimean Tatars. Tbilisi is the only one not on a coast, but two seas still play an essential role in its cosmopolitan histories and aspirations: the Caspian and Black Seas. Tbilisi owes it importance since the early middle ages to a western branch of the Silk Road, to an overland road connecting the two seas, connecting Eastern Europe (and for a long time the Byzantine empire) to Central Asia.

Each of these cities is aware of a cosmopolitan past, has a complex history of positioning itself vis-a-vis that past, and a series of attempts to revive what is perceived to be a somehow superior past. In each case, counter-discourses exist, nationalist, localist and otherwise. Each had a cosmopolitan history in which this cosmopolitanism was not always appreciated, not always perceived, and rarely stable in its incarnation. We discuss each city briefly in terms of narrative dynamics, networks and governance, teasing out elements for a theory of cosmopolitanism giving due importance to the contributions of local agency and contingency.

After these succinct and theoretically driven comparisons, we present a more extensive treatment of the various forms and functions of local cosmopolitanism in the small Romanian town of Sulina, in the Danube Delta, on the Black Sea, a place with a cosmopolitan past, and a rather marginal present, colored by stories of globally embedded pasts and futures. Sulina was important as a hub in networks that do not exist anymore, driven by agents that are not there anymore, filled with groups who disappeared, and it was governed for a century by a precursor of the European Union, the CED, Commission Europeenne du Danube, taking care of the Lower Danube area after the Crimean war (Iordachi and Van Assche 2014). A dramatic shift from centrality to marginality created a complex web of memories and aspirations, and an intriguing case to investigate local constructions and reconstructions of cosmopolitanism.

Bringing together insights from these cases, we discuss policy implications of the observed forms and functions of cosmopolitan narratives, and we discuss the implications of our local and comparative analyses for a theory of cosmopolitanism that can give due place to (a) the forces and networks at several scales enabling cosmopolitan imaginaries, (b) the semi-autonomous narrative dynamics further explaining local myths of cosmopolitanism, and (c) the varied and not necessarily cohesive functions of these narratives in a community.

These functions, we believe, can best be understood through the lens of governance. Narratives are constructed, adopted, transformed in governance arena's, and the co-evolution of actors and institutions, of power and knowledge, of formal and informal institutions in governance configurations helps to explain the manifestations of cosmopolitanism. Governance, we will show, is a process of self-reference and self-transformation, and it is the place where questions of local identity and relations to larger wholes become more pregnant, since potentially influencing collectively binding decisions.

Thus, our approach can contribute to theories of globalization and global/local interaction, bringing the local discursive mechanics into sharper focus than usual, and also adding to the scala of existing theories by emphasizing the semi-autonomous character of narrative constructions of self and community in a larger world, not entirely determined by one spatial scale, not entirely determined by economic forces, nor discursive dynamics. What brings the exact nature of that semi-autonomy sharper into focus is the embedding in governance newly understood, and the reliance on both theoretical and empirical explorations.

We believe the volume has something to offer anthropologists, political scientists, policy and governance studies, geographers, and philosophers. It will enrich the literature on cosmopolitanism but also on local governance and narrative dynamics. The research is grounded, in ten years of fieldwork (since 2003), in Sulina and the surrounding marshlands of the Danube delta, in Tbilisi, and to a lesser extent in Odessa. For Trieste, we rely on secondary literature. That research has led already to a series of publications, some of them more accessible than others, some of them in Romanian, some offering partial syntheses of the topics present in this book.

This volume offered us and offers the readers an opportunity to see these investigations in their full form and articulated complexity, at a stage when it became possible to derive broader ideas, to contribute to the larger discussions mentioned earlier in this introduction.

References

Delanty G (2009) The cosmopolitan imagination. The renewal of critical social theory. Cambridge University Press, Cambridge

Iordachi C, Van Assche K (eds) (2014) The biopolitics of the Danube Delta. Lexington/Rowman & Littlefield, Lanham

Luhmann N (1990) Political theory and the welfare state. Walter de Gruyter, Berlin

Van Assche K, Beunen R, Duineveld M (2014) Evolutionary governance theory: an introduction. Springer, Berlin

Part II
A Broader Angle

Chapter 2
A Brief Orientation in the Literature

Abstract In this chapter, we position ourselves succinctly in the vast literature on cosmopolitanism, which is recently linked to discussions of globalization, seen as something new, but which has a history of its own, as a concept, a figure, a set of practices, an epithet for places and communities. We acknowledge the practical importance in politics and moral life of continuing the discussions about diversity in a world of new mobilities, connections and coexistences, but for our present purposes take a distance from normative stances and plan to investigate cosmopolitan places as communities believing in a special relationship between themselves and the larger world, a relationship which affects the linkages between past, present and future locally and which in the final analysis is always a local product.

Keywords Globalization · Cosmopolitanism · Mobilities · Social memory · Literature · Image of unity

The academic interest in cosmopolitanism in recent years reflects this complex history. Some authors take sides with one philosopher, other explore the history of the concept (Fine 2007), of cosmopolitan practices, some analyses are normative (e.g. most authors in Brock and Brighouses overview of the philosophy of cosmopolitanism—2005), others not (the rather brilliant Delanty 2009, hovers in between), sometimes there is a very cautious questioning (van Hooft and Vandekerckhove 2010) and in some cases one can speak of attempts to reconstruct the concept of cosmopolitanism and adapt it to new modes of coexistence, mobility and globalization (e.g. Rumford's concept of 'critical cosmopolitanism'—2008). Held (2006) and others remarked that both the narratives and practices of cosmopolitanism expected, respected and possible in communities, are tightly linked with their ideas of the good polity, the desirable model of democracy, the forms and scales of governance and identification (Benhabib et al. 2006).

Indeed, the interest in globalization in the 1990s and early 2000s sparked a re-examination of cosmopolitanism (Held and McGrew 2005 for an excellent overview of debates on the links between the two), as a more positive concept, in most academic descriptions, than globalization, most often seen in the light of a homogenizing and oppressive cosmopolitanism. We cannot engage with the full scope of this literature here, as it distracts from our own attempt to concisely reconstruct the concept from new basic distinctions. We cannot omit to position ourselves, however, and, as we already indicated, a first position we can stake out is that we take no position in the normative debate on trans-national governance, international law, universal moral obligations, and human rights. We grasp the importance of the debate, but believe it can be framed also in terms of the age old questions regarding the universality of law and the moral nature of humanity. We can only observe that the positions in the debate are re-iterated since ancient Greek times, and do not expect an answer soon. We can also observe that the disappearance of some borders and boundaries brings new ones to life, as people, as individuals and as groups, seem to have the need to define themselves by means of them (Rumford 2008; Calhoun, 2007). The more messianic versions of cosmopolitan theory, involving the abolishing of all difference, of all borders and boundaries, seem therefore a bit overblown.

Indeed, several recent authors bring the discussion of cosmopolitanism to the discussion of unity in diversity, or the acceptance of difference and similarity, or simply the acceptance of difference in a new unity, or new unities with old differences, or the value of hybridity and re-appropriation of what comes from elsewhere (Brock and Brighouse 2005). Some authors focus on mobilities, and describe the potential of people, ideas, goods, moving in new larger networks at higher speeds to de-stabilize existing unities pretending universality, but also to create new conceptual frames enabling coexistence or simply new modes of coexistence (Hall and Tucker 2004). When people move, they change, and their modes of anchoring, in groups, in history, in place. Home changes for them, as it changes for and in all cultures, despite mythologies of family, village, tribe pretending eternal validity. Making a home in a globalized world, in a cosmopolitan fashion, is for some people, and for some authors, a problem, for others not—just as for some writers the act of moving, of resettling, 'uprooting' is a problem, not for others (Duyvendak 2011; Craith 2012).

For cosmopolitanism to mean something again in political and cultural theory, we cannot reduce it to a notion of simple diversity, and we cannot reduce it to a utopian version of a smooth and friction-less world society. We acknowledge the liberating potential of modernist descriptions and experiences, present in art and academia (Berman 2001), liberating the individual from traditions, from fixed identities, from small communities with oppressive internal controls, and we acknowledge the romantic idea of the community as a nest, a home, a place of identification and a place of experiment (Thomas 2010). Neither of them is suspicious per se, but, as Romanticism and Enlightenment should be regarded as two sides of the same coin, the cosmopolitan and anti-cosmopolitan imaginations of home and self are similarly to be considered two necessary values in the ongoing conversations and experiments in and on the formation of persons and communities (Wohlgemut 2009). For both perspectives, differences can be a problem. Speaking of an other can be useful in a preliminary stage of theory formation, but brings its own brand of blinding reductionism (cf. Leonard 2005).

What interests us more than these highly relevant discussions, yet for us more relevant in the practice of politics than in academic endeavors, is the idea of cosmopolitan places, which we will try to de-couple from discourses on big cities and others striving to be big and bold and asking the help of place branding experts and starchitects to secure a place in the Real world order (Binnie et al. 2006). Small places can be cosmopolitan. Lousy architects can contribute to this. Or no architects might be involved. We want to de-couple our analysis equally from analyses of architecture, planning, place branding which relegate those to the terrain of inherently alienating practices riding the horse of the apocalypse of globalization (Cronin and Hetherington 2008). Places have had a brand for ages, and worked on branding for many centuries, and no reference to neo-liberalism is required. Places remembered and forgot, selectively, and in waves, with modernist ideologies of forgetting and replacing creating many resistant memories and not simply causing actual forgetting (Crinson 2005; Staiger et al. 2009). Place brands were always associated with narratives which included and excluded, which worked for a while, and then not, which invoked praise, and provoked resistance. Any story draws boundaries and each boundary includes and excludes (Keith 2005). One can manage boundaries, and one can invoke several competing or mutually softening boundaries. Cosmopolitanism and parochialism can coexist, and when versions of cosmopolitanism arrive on a local scene, they can induce new parochialisms (Hemelryk Donald et al. 2009).

We cannot take position in all these debates, and we believe it is utterly non-necessary, since what interests us is something different: how places, small and large, can envision themselves in a special relation with a larger whole, a unity understood as a desirable world order, in which and for which one means something. Cosmopolitanism in its broadest sense, and for us the sense most worthwhile investigating, is a relation, between a part and a whole, based on images of the whole in the part, a special relation, special because of... Empirically, one can fill in different things, and we will discuss several places, communities, where different reasons are given or implied. Memory, imagination and visions of a new future can blend easily in such narrative atmosphere of exceptionalism; the stories can drive, propel, inspire, and they can blind, veil, oppress, thwart, and make a city stumble (Nowicka and Rovisco 2009). Past, present and future enter into a different relation to each other. A cosmopolitan past is seen as worthwhile reviving, and traces of it are quickly discerned in the present, while a cosmopolitan future in line with the past, is seen as the way forward, since what was cosmopolitan then, is perceived to have a universal value (Huyssen 2003)-usually not the substance of what was universal or ahead of its time in the past, but the way of relating to a larger whole, to the world, and the capacity to navigate it, to pick its fruits and prosper in it.

A cosmopolitan past easily becomes a cosmopolitan future. A cosmopolitan present allows for other observations: the relation is often not one of centrality, but of fore-shadowing, of anticipation of an order to come (cf. Leonard 2005). That is, it might not come, but it is possible, exist in potentiality and ought to come into existence. The place participates in a world order which does not exist yet, but, barring contingent troubles, will arise, follows logically out of the patterns in the contemporary world. No individual visionaries required. The community created its own path, its internal organization and narratives allowed for a mode of functioning anticipating what is possible, and sometimes reaping the benefits. The anticipated order can be far in the future, or it can be close; it can be very different from what is known to others, or similar. It is not utopian, as cosmopolitan places are practical ones, since forced to develop in networks requiring very pragmatic adaptations (Held 2010; Nowicka and Rovisco 2009). Awareness of a special relation to the world brings often an awareness of the contingency of the world, of the fragility of the special place, often together with hybris and arrogance. Yes, this is the most wonderful and advanced place, yes, here you can really understand how the world works, but, alas, there are X and Y, empires, blind forces, conservative forces, there is ignorance and fear, and competition over power and resources. As self-awareness came with a new awareness of the world, cosmopolitan places are often more aware and self-aware. When the stories of cosmopolitanism survive, but the practices disappeared, the risks of cosmopolitanism become greater, because self-awareness can be diminished.

What this book further aims to contribute, is that cosmopolitanism is always local. This positions us further vis a vis the literature, since it is not a common assertion. Communities reproduce themselves through governance, in which narratives play various roles. Knowledge of the world, how to navigate it, of what's coming, what's important, what's universal, stories of diversity, in the world as a whole, can help to accommodate diversity internally, which can help to navigate and possibly change larger parts of the world (Delanty 2009). Success can be blinding, and motivating. A version of cosmopolitanism can become reified and ossified, can become less adaptive hence successful in the longer run. Whatever images of the whole circulate in the whole, whatever knowledge of the world is acquired by navigating it, by encountering it at home, whatever vision of the world present and future is produced at home, it will always bear the marks of home, of the community, the ways it identifies itself, its environment, its constituent parts, processes, values (Kendall et al. 2009). What cannot be understood, what cannot be valued, what cannot be decided upon, based on existing patterns of meaning, value, of decision-making, cannot transform these patterns (cf. Monterescu and Rabinowitz 2007). An expanded theory of governance sensitive to both narratives and structures of decision-making, can help to make sense of local cosmopolitanism. Later in this book, we will reframe local cosmopolitanism, and develop it, through the lens of what we call evolutionary governance theory.

References

Benhabib S et al (2006) Another cosmopolitanism. Oxford University Pres, Oxford
Berman J (2001) Modernist fiction, cosmopolitanism and the politics of community. Cambridge University Press, Cambridge
Binnie J, Holloway J, Millington S, Young C (2006) Cosmopolitan urbanism. Routledge, London
Brock G, Brighouse H (2005) The political philosophy of cosmopolitanism. Cambridge University Press, Cambridge

References

Calhoun C (2007) Nations matter. Culture, history and the cosmopolitan dream. Routledge, London

Craith M (2012) Narratives of place, belonging and language. An intercultural perspective. Palgrave, Houndmills

Crinson M (ed) (2005) Urban memory. History and amnesia in the modern city. Routledge, London

Cronin A, Hetherington K (eds) (2008) Consuming the entrepreneurial city. Image, memory, spectacle. Routledge, London

Delanty G (2009) The cosmopolitan imagination. The renewal of critical social theory. Cambridge University Press, Cambridge

Duyvendak JW (2011) The politics of home. Belonging and nostalgia in Western Europe and the United States. Palgrave, Houndmills

Fine R (2007) Cosmopolitanism. Routledge, London

Hall C, Tucker H (2004) Tourism and postcolonialism. Contested discourses, identities and representations. Routledge, London

Held D (2006) Models of democracy. Polity Press, Oxford

Held D (2010) Cosmopolitanism. Ideals and realities. Polity Press, Oxford

Held D, McGrew A (eds) (2005) The global transformations reader. An introduction to the globalization debate. Polity Press, Oxford

Hemelryk Donald S, Kofman E, Kevin C (eds) (2009) Branding cities. Cosmopolitanism, parochialism and social change. Routledge, London

Huyssen A (2003) Present pasts. Urban palimpsests and the politics of memory. Stanford University Press, Stanford

Keith M (2005) After the cosmopolitan? Multicultural cities and the future of racism. Routledge, London

Kendall G, Woodward I, Skrbis Z (2009) The sociology of cosmopolitanism. Globalization, identity, culture and government. Palgrave, Houndmills

Leonard P (2005) Nationality between poststructuralism and postcolonial theory. A new cosmopolitanism. Palgrave, Houndmills

Monterescu D, Rabinowitz D (2007) Mixed towns, trapped communities. Historical narratives, spatial dynamics, gender relations, and cultural encounters in Palestinian-Israeli towns. Ashgate, Aldershot

Nowicka M, Rovisco M (eds) (2009) Cosmopolitanism in practice. Ashgate, Aldershot

Rumford C (2008) Cosmopolitan spaces. Europe, globalization, theory. Routledge, London

Staiger U, Steiner H, Webber A (eds) (2009) Memory culture and the contemporary city. Palgrave, Houndmills

Thomas A (2010) Prague palimpsest. Writing, memory and the city. University of Chicago Press, Chicago

van Hooft S, Vandekerckhove W (eds) (2010) Questioning cosmopolitanism. Springer, Berlin

Wohlgemut E (2009) Romantic cosmopolitanism. Palgrave, Houndmills

Chapter 3
Cosmopolitanism in the Light of Philosophical Tradition

Abstract In this chapter we succinctly map the philosophical antecedents of discourses on cosmopolitanism. We pay special attention to the Enlightenment thinkers, and their variations in conceptions of cosmopolitan ideals. Without aiming at a full historical reconstruction, we jump from the Enlightenment thinkers, who offered in our view a mapping of the major philosophical positions, over a few more recent stepping stones to a post-structuralist concept of cosmopolitanism which will inspire the further reasoning towards local cosmopolitanism and its embedding in evolving governance.

Keywords Cosmopolitanism · Philosophy · Enlightenment · Universals · Narrative · Network · Post-structuralism · Narratives of difference and homogeneity

The world was a large place in the past, but not a place refusing conceptualization. Before the recent proliferation of contacts and network links connecting the most remote corners of the planet, travel and exchange took place and people had an idea of the world. Cosmologies and cosmographies went hand in hand in many cultures, offering a version of the world inextricably linked to stories of its genesis. Attempts to bring the actual world together were usually attempts to bring it under one rule, religiously motivated or not. The pax Romana and pax Mongolica, and the open attitudes and expansive networks of Tang dynasty China made it easier to travel, to meet other people and get acquainted with their customs. Regimes with global aspirations made a cosmopolitan formation easier. Fragmented politics and unstable politics made traveling tougher, yet images of the whole were nevertheless produced, and one could still be cosmopolitan in a different sense, if one assumed the rest to be the same, or if one thought the observed environment or its spiritual substructure was exemplary of a universal world order: what we see is what God intended the world to be. In a Platonic, neo-Platonic, or early Christian world view, participating in universals was mainly avoiding pitfalls in the observable realm, avoiding mortal sins or misunderstandings, so one could be rewarded later by subsumption in the true realities of an afterlife which was clearly not regionalized. The aspired-to relation to universals was not a relation to a world understood more as a whole, leaning on more personal knowledge or experience.

Yet in the same middle ages, exploration started, trade revived, cities as self-organizing entities were invented (not reinvented), trade networks competed with the emerging nation-states, and even among traveling monks, a new sense of individuality and reflexive approach to a world as unity-in-diversity can be traced. The famous ascent of Mont Ventoux by Petrarca in the early 14th century, an event enabling him to see the world from a unified perspective, as landscape, was not an isolated event, and took place in a world more connected by travel, trade and learning, with both people and places seeing themselves as more or less participating in this even tighter woven web of relations.

For the Renaissance thinkers, religion did not necessarily erode, and the individual did not render community superfluous, but in literature, arts, sciences and in the practical politics described by some of the theorists, the relation between individual and society was redefined, in conjunction with a redefinition of the influence of the individual on fate, opening more space for individual intervention, for self-invention, for individual pathways to identity and success (Mansfield 2001). One could not predict all the vagaries of life, but one could prepare; in Machiavellian terms, one cannot predict the storm, but one can build levies and bridges across the river. Fate was not a coin tossed for us, but a coin standing on its side, susceptible for a push in a desired direction. Relations to authority had to be examined, yet some authority had to be expected. For Niccolo Machiavelli, Renaissance man par excellence, these and other considerations brought him to plea for a unification of Italy (300 years before it actually happened), and a plea for a world government, in which strife between polities would not structurally distract from striving towards the common good.

The Renaissance saw a re-emergence of utopian genres of art and literature (More, Campanella, Della Mirandola and others), describing perfect societies which were not only u-topian in the sense of impossible, not existing yet, but also in the sense of freed from place and community ties. Utopia is cosmopolitan, and the later appearing negative inversion, dystopia, ought to be regarded similarly as cosmopolitan, despite the occasional reference to regimes despised by the author. Utopia and dystopia ultimately refer to a human condition sliding deteriorating or possibly improvable, but universal. For Machiavelli, utopia could be imagined but simply presenting it as a moral lesson without a practicable way forward, without a path to get there, was a waste of time. World society as an objective required detailed analysis of factional politics and conflicting polities, since such analysis could illuminate the obstacles and hence possible ways to overcome them.

Machiavelli did not believe in natural law, as providing an order of universal rights which could structure a world society. Good laws were adaptable laws, and world society was not something to aspire to because it embodied a universal and morally superior order, but because it took away obstacles for society to decide on common goals and goods, to order them and to adapt them to changing internal and external environments. For the Renaissance neo-Platonists (such as Pico della Mirandola), such order did exist, and some saw it approachable in politics, while others still placed it in the afterlife or a parallel universe.

With Locke and Montesquieu, the emphasis on individual freedoms and natural rights more broadly came to the fore in the scientific reflection on politics, and simultaneously the idea of perfectibility became more entrenched (Held 2006). In the Enlightenment reflection on perfect societies, they came to look more and more possible, since natural rights could provide a universal frame which could be achieved, and science and rationality could assist in discovering obstacles, practical and cognitive, and in removing those obstacles. Maybe a revolution was necessary, maybe not. For some, the substance of perfect society could be sketched out, for others, the universal order to strive for was more procedural. For Rousseau, cosmopolitanism was only positive as a return to a human nature of sentiments and small communities, a return to localized modes of living and being which nevertheless improved the sense of unity and belonging to humanity. Traveling would not bring a deeper experience of the world by seeing diversity, but by coming closer to the universals of the heart.

For Voltaire, meanwhile, traveling and participating in politics everywhere presented splendid opportunities to learn, like Machiavelli, about both particulars and universals, and he observed a world which became more interconnected, a world where leaders in politics, business and science were learning from each other, but also a world elite still very good at fooling themselves and following the fashions of the day. For Voltaire, as for Machiavelli earlier, leadership cannot be omitted from the equation, cannot be missed on a path towards a more enlightened and thus more unified world. Leadership in politics can require despotism (a functional equivalent to popular revolution, bringing change while breaking the existing rules and ideal principles). Leadership in culture, science, business, requires a cosmopolitan attitude, a membership in an elite capable of traveling, learning, comparing, absorbing impressions and finding the universals present and absent. Without cosmopolitan elite leadership, world society would not emerge.

For Kant, the search for universals had to follow different paths, which could later be merged again. Kant believed in world society, and thought this could come about by a reflection on the preconditions of rational reasoning (searching for the conditions of truth finding), of ethical reasoning (the process of distinguishing good and bad), and an understanding of judgment (in a 'case study' of esthetic judgment, the assessment of beauty, the most difficult form of judgment). Kant did not travel far from Konigsberg, but read voraciously on every place and topic imaginable, and this cosmopolitanism of the mind informed his quest for world society, his investigation of the unified conditions for diversity in morals, manners and beliefs. He did not see cosmopolitanism as an ideal of homogeneity, but rather an understanding of diversity in a new light, with a new ability to distinguish correct from incorrect, moral from immoral and appropriate from not appropriate.

Hegel, two generations later, saw world society in a much more substantive way. For him, the unity of the world was always there, but not visible for the sentient creatures of the world. It took an initial split of matter and mind, and later an evolution of the mind and of political entities, towards science and enlightenment, to grasp the unity of mind and matter, to understand that a world Spirit of universal principles pervaded everything. Hegel was initially a fan of Napoleon, as the bringer of enlightenment to the rest of the world, the establisher of a political order which could perfectly represent a new level of reflexivity and a new level of unity. Cosmopolitanism thus required political unification, but, again, intellectuals could pave the way, through their earlier understanding of unity. Such cosmopolitanism could bring closer the end of history, a final perfect state of society (Wohlgemut 2009).

In the socialism of Marx, leaning on Hegel, such final state was also imagined, but perfection in his case was a global communist society, where the workers were not alienated anymore from the products of their labor, where equality reigned, where the world of high culture was not distorting the realities of economic relations anymore. Socialism was ideally globalized, but the activists and socialist revolutionaries had to be carefully distinguished from 'bourgeois cosmopolitans', representative of a capitalist order which was also globalizing, accompanied by a set of values, beliefs and attitudes equally bourgeois. In the early USSR, international was good, cosmopolitan bad, yet, de facto, a layer of society developed which was intellectual in orientation, and overlapping with the power elite. The 'intelligentsia' was not completely aware of what was going on in the west, but was interested, and played a role of internal semi-accepted critic of the regime, a trigger for slow adaptation and improvement (even when such was theoretically impossible in the Soviet ideology). Soviet internationalism was about spreading communist ideology and power, aided by its cultural products; but it was wary of open confrontation and comparison (Humphrey 2004). The ideological polarization made this unthinkable.

Where socialism took hold, in Russia, the industrial revolution had not truly taken place. Except for a few small regions, there were no factories, and no proletarians to carry the revolution forward. The proletarian was itself a cosmopolitan figure, an entity produced by globalizing capitalism, and an enabler for a next step in globalization, towards socialism. This proletarian had to be created in the Soviet Union, an intermediate product of a planned transformation of society. The proletarian was himself not an intellectual, not well travelled, but a new entity on a road of objective history towards an objectively superior and unified whole.

The place where socialism in practice was born, was on a margin, a margin produced by lack of investment, by conservative politics in Russia, but also by the European imagination of the 18th Century. 'Eastern Europe' became 'backward', despotic, and oriental when the Enlightenment took off in Western Europe, and these images did not significantly change when the Central European Habsburg monarchy adopted some Enlightenment values and started to look at its own Eastern territories in the same way (Wolff 1994). Similar perceptions of marginality and backwardness were of course not limited to this region. Europe looked at the rest of the world in similar terms, terms driving and driven by a process of colonial expansion. In the 18th and 19th Centuries, cosmopolitanism then required an acquaintance with not only the big cities of the world, the enlightened parts of the world partaking in a process of learning and mirroring, but also with the world of colonies and places waiting to be colonized (Delanty 2009; Fine 2007).

The learned traveler appeared in different versions, some more rough than others, and the figure of the traveler could come home to be cosmopolitan, or stay in the colonies, being cosmopolitan, and pushing the progress of the colony. In the era of colonization, the European powers were of course not all alike. Each country had its own mode of operating, its own idea of the relation between colony and motherland, and of the role of the colonizing power in the world order. Similarly, some form of self-ascription as a civilizing power could be observed in many cases, but the idea of civilization was different, the set of core values and practices supposed to bring progress, and the ones to aspire to.

This being said, we have to be careful not to reduce European images of cosmopolitanism to a history of Enlightenment and a simple coupling with colonialism exporting supposedly universal Enlightenment values. We have, e.g., to distinguish other enlightenment discourses highlighting the value of being exposed as an individual to other places and people, as being exposed to difference, rather than universal ideas, ideals or practices. The German and arguably European idea of *bildung,* and the English, later European *grand tour,* can both be understood as an exposure to learning/seeing of classic examples, of universal qualities to study and emulate, but also as a profoundly *personal* mix of learning and experience, of authors, topics, places and events (Black 2003). Places show up as places to learn about, the locations of great battles, and the homes of great writers, but also as places to visit, the two categories overlapping and offering an extra impetus for learning and travel. *Bildung* was not only an encyclopedic acquiring of knowledge, but a personal route through the landscape of learning and culture, blending personal traits and elements of pre-existing knowledge. The trip to Europe and possibly the Middle East recommended to well-off youth was not only intended to bring them into contact with the classics; it was an opportunity to grow up through contact with different people and places (Bruford 1975). A certain level of tension, conflict and transgression of common norms was expected.

Places can become cosmopolitan then in different, paradoxical manners. If people can become cosmopolitan by encounters with a canon of timeless classics, in discursive and physical worlds, and by accumulating experiences of difference, and becoming different (individual), then one can expect something similar for places. We would indeed say that places can become cosmopolitan by becoming the same, that is, similar to other cosmopolitan places somehow in the fore-front of a world order only shimmering through, and by accommodating difference, by a rich history leading to a unique identity. Cosmopolitan places are somehow part of a league of cosmopolitan places, similar to them yet different, and the difference has to be describable as a place identity reflecting a history of encounters and a current set of encounters and differences. The encounters can take place in and thanks to a global network of relations, and they can result from an internal diversity, a collection of elements each with their own expansive network, making the place a node, a hub (Binnie et al. 2006). Similarity with other cosmopolitan places in that case comes with the hub-character, each similar place expected to be a similar crossroads of networks, and, if the groups with the networks have a long history, a crossroads of histories (Rumford 2008).

Internal diversity can be ethnic and cultural diversity, but not necessarily. It can be political diversity, economic diversity, a class structure, a diversity of roles combining economic and political aspects, a diversity simply of networks, of lifestyles (nomadic, settled, urban, rural, local, traveling). Ethnicity cannot be considered the grounding factor here; it can come first and it can come after taking a position in another web of differences (Benhabib et al. 2006; Held 2010). A 'Greek' could come from current Greece, he could be Greek because of his family, and thus become a merchant, or he could become Greek by entering a merchant class in a city somewhere around the Black Sea. Or he could become Greek by entering a merchant network spanning the Black Sea area. One category of difference cannot take precedence in general; per place and time, different layers of difference overlap, and ground each other in differing patterns.

We'd like to highlight the concept of *network* here. Networks always existed, as connections of links between people, places, knowledge, allowing for the formation of hubs, of nodes, of higher densities, of overlaps, and, most importantly, allowing for moving, learning and exchange. Networks allow for movement in different directions; there are different paths towards one location and one can often find effects of actions, movements and exchanges in various unexpected places in the network, because of effects rippling through the fabric of connections (Fuchs 2001). Early network metaphors can be traced centuries back: cosmopolitanism as participation to different degrees in large scale and dynamic networks. 'Backwaters' and 'backward groups and individuals' can also in this metaphor be opposed to cosmopolitan places, groups and individuals, since they do not participate in higher level networks, but either by choice or tradition or accident remain confined to smaller and less dynamic networks (Shields 1994). Eastern Europe was considered a backwater also because few universities existed, few literary salons, few awe-inspiring entrepreneurs (Wolff 1994).

A second concept to give central place, we believe, is *narrative dynamics*. Places and people can be cosmopolitan in practice, in the navigation of larger networks in spatial and conceptual terms. Yet the different versions of cosmopolitanism are in essence stories, narratives, on relations between the whole and the parts, parts being people and places (Van Assche et al. 2014). For the ascription of something, of a part, as cosmopolitan, they rely on other stories, by others. For the self-ascription as cosmopolitan, an accumulation of stories and storied journeys cannot be missed. And the description of a person or place as cosmopolitan by others usually relies on a reference to stories, to a history of stories and to an openness for a diversity of stories and for new stories, coming with a position at an intersection of people, places, discourses (Held and McGrew 2005).

The philosophical versions of cosmopolitanism, we believe, are only partly connected to their historical and cultural contexts. Philosophers were formed by their time and space, but also refer back and make sense in a philosophical tradition, which can be understood as a long debate with an ever growing line of predecessors. In the Enlightenment, a particular nexus emerged between culture, politics and philosophy, in which one could be seen to ground the other. But this is not always the case, and our brief encounter with the Romantics already revealed this. A tangle of discourses developed on cosmopolitanism, revolving around a central tension between unity and difference, around a unique path to membership in a club of current specials and future not-so-specials (Fine 2007; Brock and Brighouse 2005). Cosmopolitanism cannot miss however a reference to unity, to a spatial and cultural unity which can be better represented by some. From there, things start to differ, between discourses on cosmopolitan people, places, cultures.

European cultural history offers a wide variety of discourses on cosmopolitan figures and places. In literature, the origins of these figures can be literary and non-literary. The traveler becomes slowly not a lost figure, not a person out of place, but a representative of a new world (Black 2003). Places become slowly not problematic because mixed, but interesting and representative because of the mix and the associated connectivity; or they become not despised because rapidly changing, but revered because of a rapidly crystallizing modernity (Held and McGrew 2005). History too, becomes ambiguous then, depending on the nature of the world order and its relation with the past: if that desirable order to participate in is felt as a radical break with the past, or a past, then a long history can be an obstacle for cosmopolitanism, whereas a new order emerging organically out of the old one, and reusing elements and insights, can lean on a long history and present it as a hallmark of cosmopolitanism. A new order shedding a legacy of religious politics can emphatically try to shed a network of religious ideas and organizations spanning the globe and many centuries, while highlighting a rebirth under a new banner or highlighting a different history and associated networks: trade, arts, civic self-organization.

The cosmopolitan person can be a product of the cosmopolitan place and the other way around. Following the line of distinction between *Bildung* and *grand tour*, the emphasis can be on a *vita activa* and a *vita contemplativa* (Bruford 1975; Black 2003; Magris 2011). Voltaire can represent the active navigation and construction of cosmopolitan networks and values, while Kant was probably more comfortable exploring and expanding the discursive universe of an 18th century Europe constructing modernity and cosmopolitanism. As many others have pointed out, Enlightenment and Romanticism ought not to be seen as opposites or simply reactions to each other (Wohlgemut 2009; Gay 1981). They co-existed from the beginning, often within the same circles and places, and can best be analyzed as aspects of the same movement. Such more complex analysis can illuminate the complexities of the romantic and post-romantic literary and practical cosmopolitans—the writers and their literary creations, their vagaries, and the increasingly frenetic travel and connectivity of their world.

A multitude of entwining, overlapping and sometimes contradicting discourses of cosmopolitanism appears both in 19th century literature and in the world at large. Some characters are men of the world, as in traveling merchants, diplomats, others are more vaguely defined travelers, in the service of others or independent, still others stay at home but participate in the activities enabled by international networks, and finally, there are intellectual and artistic cosmopolitans who only want to know about other places, benefit from the best of these places, partly model their behavior after what is thought to happen elsewhere. The figure of Casanova, always in trouble but unproblematic as a representative of cosmopolitan circles, was an 18th century figure. One could say that the tensions between Romanticism and

Enlightenment present from the early 18th century were explored and magnified and became visible in next generations, and led to the perception of an opposition between particular and universal, local and global, between emotion and rationality, between moderation and excess, a perception missing its underlying structure: the configuration of Romanticism and Enlightenment represented a matrix of all these possibilities, with a version of the world, of rationality, of moderation, and versions of cosmopolitanism part and parcel of discourses described as Romantic.

Moderation became more meaningful in the presence of the possibility of excess, of deeply felt motivations for moderation, rationality could be cold and warm, and emotions could be misguided (Gay 1981). Localism could similarly be undesirable (when e.g. simply continuing tradition), and history and tradition were appreciated only in the light of a new reflexivity which smuggled in immediately new concepts of rationality and of a desirable world order, in which certain traditions, certain forms of localism and certain schemes of emotion were acceptable and interesting for a well educated person belonging to respected classes. Romantics were globalists as well, and they are representatives of the same push towards reflexivity, specialization and complexity we commonly ascribe to the Enlightenment. More simplistically: Modernism was Enlightenment + Romanticism and cosmopolitanism is a product of such inherently ambiguous discursive configuration.

Versions of cosmopolitanism acquire a hierarchical ordering in society, with some forms of activity and some forms of reflection being more recognized as valuable and 'cosmopolitan' than others (Kofman 2005; Kendall et al. 2009). The Romantic era was also the age of Nationalism, partly a counterforce to the universalizing forces of large bureaucratic modernizing empires and of industrial revolution and to the mere fact of rapid change. But not entirely a reactionary counter force. We should not be blind to the fact that what spread across Europe and later the colonies was a unified theory of nationalism as cosmopolitan product of the European Enlightenment: Culture = Language = Nation $\Longrightarrow$ Nation as political entity. The idea of natural rights appertaining to a language group defined as ethnic group and expected to achieve self-determination through the creation of a nation state, that idea was an idea, a discursive creation (Magris 2011). It was understood as a universal formula, linking an objective determination of group identity to an objectively superior and more appropriate form of political organization. What spread in an expanding network of media, merchandise and politics was a homogenous and homogenizing narrative, in this case a narrative of difference, uniqueness and authenticity.

Under the influence of the nationalist formula, places were supposed to be labelled in national/ethnic terms more than before, and polities such as the Habsburg, Ottoman and Russian empires and their forms of cosmopolitanism immediately started to look unnatural, unauthentic and potentially oppressive (Magris 2011). Cosmopolitan places could be national capitals, representing best the identity of the nation, yet participating clearly in a modernity all nations were expected to strive for. In some cases, where those capitals stayed multi-ethnic, this could be a sign of the attractiveness of the place for others, a sign of cosmopolitanism, but also an ongoing friction with narratives of national unity and identity (Binnie et al. 2006; Kendall et al. 2009). Where histories of nationalism and centralization of power de facto cut network ties, and either assimilated 'minorities' or pushed them out, the memory of diversity, and the physical signs of that former diversity (buildings, food, music,...) could now safely be presented as a proof of cosmopolitanism, without actually having to deal with these absent differences. So many places proudly show their Jewish, Armenian, Greek quarters, admitting after a while that the Jews, Armenians, Greeks, left a long time ago (Mills 2006).

Persons aspiring to be cosmopolitan in the context of nationalism and nation states can still fall under the different categories mentioned before. They can be in places offering a privileged spectacle of modern life, possibly of a density of networks and diversity, can read about modernity and diversity, and they can travel. Travel for diversity and unity, for a cosmopolitan formation, then becomes traveling for encounters with many of the recognized building blocks of cultural and political life, with many 'authentic' ethnic groups, with and without a state, comparing them, reflecting on their state vis a vis the formula of nationalism and experiencing their common humanity and shared desire towards progress (Held and McGrew 2005). Reading and traveling and residing in a hub increases cosmopolitan respectability.

One can thus speak of homogenizing narratives of differences, and of differing narratives of homogeneity. Both network dynamics and narrative dynamics can exert forces of homogenization on communities, yet in each case, counter forces can be observed. We emphasize that this force/counterforce distinction is not the same as the global/local distinction. There are other forces emanating from the global or international level, and there are other local forces, and each side of our distinction can be tied to both local and global.

In order to address local/global dynamics, and fit it into our developing theoretical frame, we speak of *local cosmopolitanism*, of local constructions and functions of cosmopolitanism. These local constructions are not simply counter-forces to discourses of similarity and differences that emanated in global networks. At this point, we can already say that the ammunition for creating images of self as local and global, as similar and different to others in the same place and to other places, is a product of local and global discourses, literary and non-literary. The images of the local can be derived from global narratives, and the images of the global can be locally constructed. What we call local cosmopolitanism is this whole process of negotiation at the local level of both local and global, utilizing discursive elements *and strategies*, that have both local and global origins. In the next chapters, analyzing the fine mechanics of local cosmopolitanism, we scrutinize this process of negotiation and further develop our theory of local cosmopolitanism.

References

Benhabib S et al (2006) Another cosmopolitanism. Oxford University Pres, Oxford
Binnie J, Holloway J, Millington S, Young C (2006) Cosmopolitan urbanism. Routledge, London
Black J (2003) Italy and the grand tour. Yale University Press, New Haven

Brock G, Brighouse H (2005) The political philosophy of cosmopolitanism. Cambridge University Press, Cambridge

Bruford W (1975) The German tradition of self-cultivation: bildung from Humboldt to Thomas Mann. Cambridge University Press, Cambridge

Delanty G (2009) The cosmopolitan imagination. The renewal of critical social theory. Cambridge University Press, Cambridge

Fine R (2007) Cosmopolitanism. Routledge, London

Fuchs S (2001) Against essentialism. Cambridge University Press, Cambridge

Gay P (1981) Enlightenment, vol 1. Random House, New York

Held D (2010) Cosmopolitanism. Ideals and realities. Polity Press, Oxford

Held D (2006) Models of democracy. Polity Press, Oxford

Held D, McGrew A (eds) (2005) The global transformations reader. An introduction to the globalization debate. Polity Press, Oxford

Humphrey C (2004) Cosmopolitanism and kosmopolitizm in the political life of Soviet citizens. Focaal 2004(44):138–152

Kendall G, Woodward I, Skrbis Z (2009) The sociology of cosmopolitanism. Globalization, identity, culture and government. Palgrave, Houndmills, Basingstone

Kofman E (2005) Figures of the cosmopolitan: privileged nationals and national outsiders. Innov Eur J Soc Sc Res 18(1):83–97

Magris C (2011) Danube. Random House, New York

Mansfield HC (2001). Machiavelli's new modes and orders: a study of the Discourses on Livy. University of Chicago Press, Chicago

Mills A (2006) Boundaries of the nation in the space of the urban: landscape and social memory in Istanbul. Cult Geogr 13(3):367–394

Rumford Ch (2008) Cosmopolitan spaces. Europe, globalization, theory. Routledge, London

Shields R (1994) Places on the margin. Sage, London

Van Assche K, Beunen R, Duineveld M (2014) Evolutionary governance theory: an introduction. Springer, Heidelberg

Wohlgemut E (2009) Romantic cosmopolitanism. Palgrave, Houndmills, Basingstoke

Wolff L (1994) Inventing Eastern Europe: the map of civilization on the mind of the enlightenment. Stanford University Press, Stanford

Chapter 4
Cosmopolitanism and Networks: Odessa, Trieste, Tbilisi

Abstract In order to illustrate the interplay between networks and narratives in the construction of cosmopolitan communities, we discuss Odessa, Trieste, and Tbilisi. Each has a past that was more cosmopolitan than the present, and each, in different degrees and manners, remembers and uses that cosmopolitan past to understand its present and guide them towards its future. In each case, the cosmopolitan past is mythologized in different ways, masking less pleasant or less understandable aspects of these past societies. The current frames to remember these pasts are very different from the conceptual frames one can surmise in the cosmopolitan periods remembered/reconstructed. Each city picks different symbolic sites, practices, events, groups, story lines, to illustrate the cosmopolitan character of the past. The influence of policy and planning differed per city, as did the network dynamics that enabled rise and fall of these places. We start with an introduction of a few post-structuralist concepts which can assist us in developing our theory of local cosmopolitanism and analyze our case communities.

Keywords Cosmopolitanism · Networks · Social memory · Mythologies · Identity · Odessa · Trieste · Tbilisi · Lost centrality · Nostalgia

We believe it is fruitful to jump forwards in cultural and intellectual history to the 1960's, to France. Then and there, one can discern the origins of what we call post-structuralism, an epistemology and ontology that informed and restructured a wide variety of schools and disciplines since then, while being inspired by a variety of events in several fields. Post-structuralism is commonly understood as the final straw in the move away from modernism, from modernist ideas on truth, methods to find the truth, on universals, and on a rational basis to organize society.

For post-structuralism, and post-modernism more broadly understood, the world consists of stories, of narratives. Some are more stable than others, some ground others, some compete with others. Grounding of other stories can take place through definition of key concepts, organizational principles, metaphors. The national communities 'discovered' by Romanticism and used to anchor new or old nation states, were analyzed now as imagined communities, and national histories and traditions as invented traditions and deliberate constructions to legitimize and perpetuate dominant configurations of power/knowledge. Historians finding the 'facts' of history were now seen as working within paradigms constructing facts and their interpretation, and serving powers that be or counter-discourses aiming to take positions of power. Aspirations of universality were analyzed as aspirations, without a ground in universals pre-existing those aspirations.

Personal identity became likewise seen as a narrative construction, a history of experiences mediated through story-telling about self, others, and of others about oneself (Somers 1994; Hinchman and Hinchman 1997). History was deconstructed and tied to social groups representing themselves and defining themselves and to power relations assumed and reinforced. Place looked differently as well, in early versions of post-structuralism compared to text, in later versions understood as a sign system in and by itself, and as a sign system with a central role of indexicality, or contiguity, a relation between sign and concept which cannot ignore immediate proximity, as an immediate cause or a touching in space (Van Assche 2004). Both forms of contiguity assume a link with the material world different from other sign systems. Space was the gate through which post-structuralism brought back embodiment and materiality, in geography, anthropology, sociology, cultural studies.

Meanwhile, these theoretical developments did not signify that the real world legacies of modernism disappeared or can be discounted. Post-modern theory is perfectly compatible with a world operating mostly on modernist principles. This is the case because of the performativity, or reality effects, of modernist mythologies, and it is true because post-modern epistemology is a product of broader modernist currents allowing for new levels of reflexivity (Van Assche et al. 2012; Bal 2002). The new forms of unity in the world, through expanding and densifying networks, through specialization but in similar directions across the world, through functional differentiation, all these did not disappear with the arrival of a new form of reflection called post-structuralism (Luhmann 1995). People, including theorists, could still think of unity in diversity, of places and people in the forefront, or simply more interesting, of experiences bestowing an aura of cosmopolitanism.

Theory needs to reckon with this, certainly a theory of cosmopolitanism. We need a conceptual place to compare the various concepts and metaphorical understandings of cosmopolitanism in a post-modern era. We can start by distinguishing between networks and narratives, each marked by their dynamics. Networks can then refer to the modernist world of globalization and cosmopolitan practices can be understood as engaging in the process and learning about places where it is intense and observable. Narratives can then be the realm of post-modern reflection, the appearance of identities and histories for the second-order observer, the observer of observations others make, of the stories they tell about themselves and the world. Indeed, identities can be seen as narrative constructions, and social and spatial identities can refer to the world at large in various manners. Each social identity can produce a different world it belongs to, and a different idea of ideally relating to it or representing it. Social identities produce their own cosmopolitanism (Mills 2006; Van Assche et al. 2009b).

Yet, such distinction is not enough. Not all narratives are possible. They are limited in their shape and impact by other narratives, by larger narratives (discursive configurations) and by the material world, its physical properties, its power relations, its networks (Fuchs 2001; Van Assche et al. 2014). Network dynamics does not determine but constrains narrative dynamics. Global networks do not produce but can enable or induce narratives of globalization or of cosmopolitanism. They can also articulate as cosmopolitan that what happens in large scale networks, or what resembles it, or that what profits from these networks, where the benefits trickle down and the collected expertise condensates.

We can follow Bruno Latour and Stephan Fuchs on networks, and see networks as discursive infrastructures, topological structures where knowledge and power are created and circulated (Fuchs 2001). Narrative/network becomes a different distinction then. The reality of neither is placed higher on a ladder of truth or proximity to a Real, and networks and narratives are two aspects of a system of knowledge/power which transforms as a result of its own contingent operations. The world and its stories are and remain the result of networks. It remains necessary, we believe, to see a difference between sorts of networks, and several typologies can be useful. One can, with Fuchs and Luhmann, distinguish networks with different functions (legal, political, economic, scientific). But one can also distinguish networks tied to other forms of differentiation, e.g. to segmentary differentiation, to ethnic and social groups (cf Luhmann 1995). Globalization as a manifestation of a still unfolding modernity can be diagnosed through the analysis of the functional networks, and can be understood as the result of these proliferating and subdividing networks. While within certain academic (scientific) networks, new forms of reflexivity can develop which deconstruct the assumptions that ignited those modernist developments a few centuries ago.

In order to create a new space for contingency, we borrow from Deleuze and geographers inspired by him (e.g. Massey 2005; Thrift 2005) a concept of place as confluence of stories. Those stories can alter by meeting others in place, and they can modify the nature of the place, its identity, where stories meet and modify in a pattern determined by the stories, the mode of encounter, the physical characteristics, the speed and rhythm, and last not but least the memories of other places and encounters and stories which are never entirely gone, but constitute a virtual realm capable of re-emerging and re-combining with new elements. Such concept is only incompatible with the most rigid of network concepts. In fact, we can re-imagine networks through Deleuze, as including spaces, people and stories in one network, actual and virtual, and imagining an extreme susceptibility of each element to change caused by other elements of different natures (cf Thrift 2005). A Deleuzian rhizome is a network. In line again with Deleuze, we would say that the material world, of matter and power, is not a product of the discursive, of knowledge and power, and that the discursive and the material cannot ignore each other. This is not merely a matter of resistance to each other, but of co-creation, of discursive and material elements coming together to create something that comes within the grasp of people, and becomes productive, creating new discourses and materialities (Deleuze and Guattari 1987).

The world looks like a rather fluid place in such perspective. It is a place where some discursive structures and power structures can persist however for a long time. Cosmopolitanism can still be seen as being representative of the more rigid large scale networks underpinned by shared realities (similar to the molarity concept with Deleuze) but it can also be a feature of a person or place more aware than others of the fluidity and its patterns, its modes of transformation. Cosmopolitanism in that sense can represent a higher level of creativity, of sensibility, after removing rigid mythologies of unity, history and identity (Delanty 2009). And it remains possible to reconstruct the modes of cosmopolitanism marking particular networks as products of those networks, as products of the confluence of local and global narratives in a place, subjected to its own rule of transformation.

We will further develop these ideas in the analysis of cosmopolitan places in this and later chapters. We take a closer look now at places with a cosmopolitan past and a recurring nostalgia for it: Trieste, Tbilisi and Odessa. Nostalgia produces reinterpretations of the past, and new versions of the cosmopolitan narrative (Della Dora 2006). Places like these, formerly in the center and aware of it, and later relegated to more marginal positions, equally aware, present us with important material to study variants of cosmopolitanism, and of the relation between networks and narratives, past and present, and the current powers of virtual pasts. They are also interesting places to look for continuity and discontinuity in cosmopolitan narratives locally, and to look at the role of local networks, discourses and practices in this relation.

A vague feeling of being apart from a *topos* invested with personal affection, longing for or having lost such a *topos*, nostalgia is, more than anything, related to space and place. "Nostalgia as a feeling arises from place in two ways: from its idealized image in the geographical imagination of the individual (or of a community), but also from 'material' topographical features (like landmarks or buildings), objects and even names. In order to chart 'space on time and time on space' and hinder 'the distinction between object and subject', nostalgia draws by handfuls from the vast repertoire of symbols and signs which constitutes territory" (Della Dora 2006: 211).

Boym distinguishes between at least two threads of nostalgia: a "restorative" nostalgia, focusing "on *nostos* and aims to reconstruct the lost home, often in association with religious or nationalist revivals" and "reflective nostalgia" which "dwells on *algia*, and has no place of habitation. It is embodied in the essence of movement, not destination. If restorative nostalgia ends up reconstructing emblems and rituals of home and homeland in an attempt to conquer and spatialize time, reflective nostalgia cherishes shattered fragments of memory and temporalizes space" (Legg 2004: 100); it "lingers on ruins, on the patina of time and history, on uncanny silences and absences and on dreams" (Della Dora 2006: 210). Nostalgia is not only a benign feeling, set off by autobiographical details, but tends to be employed for political (in the large sense of the word) purposes.

"The emotive capacity of nostalgia gives it the future (rather than just the past) relevance that explains its recurrent manipulation as a political tool" (Legg 2004: 100). In a similar vein, Della Dora (2006; p. 100) writing about Alexandria, argues that "nostalgia can be both a powerful political weapon and an active force subverting the political as it moulds literary and material cityscapes".

Most importantly, nostalgia is connected to present in that, as David Lowenthal reminded us, in some cases "both nostalgia and heritage rely on interpretations of history to compensate for a present malaise, for a lack of community and a need for identity in place" (Mills 2006: 371). When the present is not satisfying enough, when the strength of a community is fading or the group decides to invest in a novel project for the future, revolving to the past and producing a favorable narrative of it turns nostalgia into a programmatic community assignment. And, as Irwin-Zarecka pertinently observes, "often, it is the telling itself, the ongoing articulation of the 'reality of the past' that forms and informs a community. For that matter, the past so told need not be real at all to offer the basis for communal solidarity. All that is needed is active remembrance, communally shared and deemed important for the community's self-definition" (Irwin-Zarecka 1994: 57).

Now, what about these nostalgic places full of cosmopolitan dreams?

4.1 Trieste

Trieste is probably the most analyzed of the three, and a cause celebre of early cosmopolitanism, under the flag of the Habsburg Empire, for which it was the only harbor for a long time. Trieste had been a Habsburg possession since the 14th century, and the Habsburgs opened the city for various trading minorities, among which a significant Jewish population. The lingua Franca for all minorities was a Venetian Italian dialect, and the local elite could define its unity in diversity by reference to this dialect and to a tradition of self-governance (Minca 2009). In the early 18th century, it became a free port, a free trade zone, and while it lost that status under the same Habsburgs in the 19th century, the Austrian government compensated by heavy investment in infrastructure and support for shipping and insurance companies, enabling it to maintain a status as international hub (Magris 2011). In the 18th century, local elites, old and new, aligned directly with the Habsburg policy of expansion and internationalization for Trieste, but when tensions arose, on and off until its annexation by Italy after World War I, a new identity was created, referring to the old self-governance under an elite which did not exist anymore.

In the last Habsburg decades, the Slovenian question became more important. While the attractiveness of identification with the Habsburg monarchy diminished, because of internal divisions gaining prominence, Italy became an attractor, after its unification in 1860 and after the previous 'loss' of Venice and the Veneto. Trieste felt more Italian, yet cosmopolitan. The previous mix of groups was merged into that Italian identity, but the Slovenians, always there, always on the margin, for a while not clearly identifying, came closer to the center and resisted integration (Morris 2002). The 'nationality question' in the 20th century was thus framed very simply as an Italian-Slovenian polarity, one still not entirely resolved (Fig. 4.1).

After accession to Italy, Trieste became a backwater, not fully recognized as Italian, deprived of its Central European connections, of its Eastern Mediterranean and American networks, of its internal diversity and the networks coming with that. It became a place of nostalgia, but a nostalgia that did not find an easy target. Trieste for periods of time was a center, or a center close to a bigger center (Vienna), yet now and even then, the framing of the place, its position, its identity, was problematic, according to Minca (2009) a tension which could not be resolved, leading to a famous interpretation by Jan Morris (2002) as 'nowhere'. We would say: a coexistence not of center and periphery, but of centrality and a profound non-reflection on the nature of that centrality, a non-reflection rendering it a non-place (cf Shields 1994).

Claudio Magris, a literature professor at Trieste University became world famous with his kaleidoscopic book *Danube* (2011, originally published in 1986), a trip from source to mouth, through time, crossing the boundaries of fiction, science and history, demonstrating that many present boundaries were not a hard in the past. The belonging of Trieste was also with a now lost Central Europe, lost after the repartitioning of Europe after World War I. Trieste was cosmopolitan in a world unrecognizable nowadays, populated with players not on the scene anymore; the tensions undermining its identity then are even harder to grasp now because of that, and a clear path of reinvention even harder to find. That is, beyond the confines of a standard Italian city narrative.

The spatial border and cultural boundaries always coexisted in Trieste, in patterns shifting with the coming and going of empires and with changing relations within them. Until 1797, neighboring Venice was independent, a former empire with still clear legacies around the Adriatic and Mediterranean. Until the 19th century, the Ottoman empire was close, dangerous yet offering opportunities for trade. Until the early 20th century, the Habsburg empire occupied the European heartland and had Trieste as its commercial heart. Until then, Greeks could also be Venetians and from Trieste and Slovenians could be Italians and Austrians at the same time. The changing boundaries and the changing nature of boundaries and states under influence of the seemingly simplifying formula's of nationalism, made the folding of boundaries in Trieste even more complex. Spatial boundaries became more problematic, as did cultural and ethnic ones, and the formerly internal complexity became now interpreted as external complexity plus internal ambiguity. In addition, the simplification of identities was not always accepted, and resistance of old against new created new identities and boundaries, a new complexity of identification and place not reducible to either new or old orders (Fig. 4.2).

Claudio Magris, Jan Morris and others have analyzed and celebrated Trieste cosmopolitanism, its practices and literary emanations, and others have criticized these celebrations. One can attempt to deconstruct its cosmopolitanism, by

4.1 Trieste

Fig. 4.1 Panoramic view of Trieste (around 1855). http://commons.wikimedia.org/ [Public domain]

Fig. 4.2 Vintage postcard of Trieste, Palazzo Governo (6 January 1909, dated by the sender). http://commons.wikimedia.org/ [Public domain]

pointing at the relatively limited networks, at the relatively short period of time in which it showed internal complexity and representativeness of a modernizing world, and one can deconstruct the coexistence of groups within the city, dismissing its multi-culturalism, dismissing the learning, adaptation, the synergies and compatibilities generating a city culture participating in the cult of commerce and yet distinctly Central European intellectual and still mostly Trieste (e.g. Ballinger 2003; Waley 2009). We would argue that such deconstruction is true and untrue, useful and useless: it would merely point out the obvious, that multiculturalism and multiculturalism as proof of cosmopolitanism are mythical constructs, in a present now using them and a present past where these myths had a role to play. The fact that some facts were different from the productive myth does not teach us much; it does not illuminate the productivity of the myth, its trajectory, its distinguishing features (Zizek 2008).

A feature of Triestino cosmopolitanism we find also with the others is the creation of a city myth preceding other identities. One could be first of all from Trieste, and as long as this identification would hold, an unstable political and cultural context could be held at bay, preventing from spilling over too much into internal politics and identifications (cf Driessen 2005). The city culture itself could become a distinct sign of cosmopolitanism; beyond a mere sum of internal elements there was a transformation claimed, an amalgamation not into a new national identity but into a city giving unique access to a larger world, leaning on old embeddings. For Trieste, this was the modern world, until this narrative could not hold anymore. Access was also more important than representativeness, given the unstable set of identifications mentioned before.

4.2 Odessa

Odessa is the city that is most emphatically the result of imperial policy, a creation of the Russian empire in the late 18th century, after the Tsarist armies beat the Crimean Tatars and their Ottoman overlords, and the European powers could not turn back the clock. As Trieste, the development of the city was geopolitical, but, different from Trieste, it was so from the very beginning. Russia had tried to expand southwards since the late middle ages, and Ivan IV reached the Caspian in the late 16th Century, Peter the Great the Sea of Azov in the late 17th century, but the Crimean Tatars, a group tenuously connected with the Mongol invaders of the 13th century, proved more resilient than expected and it took another century before fully 'pacify' the northern Black Sea board, and exert enough control to establish a new port and re-direct trade and development (Subtelny 2009).

The Danube became the southern border of the Russian empire, and the Tsars did not favor its trade, since it was Odessa that ought to be developed. Whereas previously, much of Ukraine was for Russia a buffer zone against the Tatars, sparsely populated and unpredictably defended by Cossacks, a new and smaller buffer was now accepted, with Cossacks, but mostly Old Believers (Staroveri,

Lipovani in the Danube delta) settling in and around the Danube delta, and other minorities a bit further. Dutch expertise was brought in to reclaim some wetlands, and turned into farmland for Russian settlers. This took place in the mid-18th century, before the full conquest of Crimea and Souther Ukraine. The Northern or Chilia branch of the Danube was already under Russian control, and lower Danube cities on that arm (such as Ismaeli and Reni) were important outlets for trade in absence of a coastal port (Richardson 2008).

Russia didn't put all its eggs in one basket, and while building Odessa, it continued its push south. Another, more southern port, and another, more strategic river, were in the cards. Although the Danube delta never officially belonged to it, it controlled the area from the late 18th to the mid 19th century. For the Ottomans, it was not important enough, and for the western powers, it only became a border deserving reinforcement after Russia tried to dismantle the whole Ottoman Empire and take over Istanbul. Only then, England and France combined forces and took Russia to task in Crimea, where it was defeated, and forced to accept the northern Danube branch as the border of the Empire, and to accept the control of the lower Danube by a new international committee, the European Danube Committee, consisting of all major European powers, but with an English and French dominance (Van Assche et al. 2009b) (Fig. 4.3).

Meanwhile, in Odessa, a Belgian engineer was attracted for the initial urban planning, but, as in Petersburg before, architects, engineers and artists from France, Italy, the Netherlands and others European countries were attracted. Foreign settlers were attracted with many benefits, ranging from tax benefits over cheap lands to semi-monopolies on certain trades and promises of state patronage and commissions (Richardson 2005, 2008). The anti-European sentiments around 1812 were a relatively brief interlude of a strongly pro-European development policy. Crimea was landscaped into a Russian Riviera, modeled after France and Italy, while Odessa was to rival not Petersburg but Southern European merchant metropoles. Viticulture was promoted with French and Italian expertise, and the classical Greek heritage was emphasized, through archaeology and new building campaigns. Classical meant Greek but also European, a sharing of the deepest roots.

Both 'European' and 'Oriental' groups settled there and transformed the city and its region. There were Armenians, Bulgarians, Greeks, Circassians, but mostly Jewish people, coming from inside and outside the Russian empire, enjoying more freedoms in Odessa than elsewhere (Subtelny 2009; Zipperstein 1982). Whereas the European groups either disappeared or were assimilated in the course of the dramatic history of the area, the Jews stayed, and cosmopolitan Odessa, for cynical later Soviet observers became 'cosmopolitan Jewish' Odessa. Odessa developed its own city culture, with people also becoming 'from Odessa', rather than first of all Russian, Ukrainian, Jewish, and inhabitants proudly wore the epithet of Odessan, associated with jokes, loud and brash behavior, smart trade, and a distinct version of cosmopolitanism (Czaplicka et al. 2009).

The 'distinct' however slowly shifted to 'distinctly Russian' and later to 'Russian', with fewer and fewer people associating with Ukraine, with the locale, with the mix. Even under the Soviets, Russification continued, and Odessa became much

4.2 Odessa

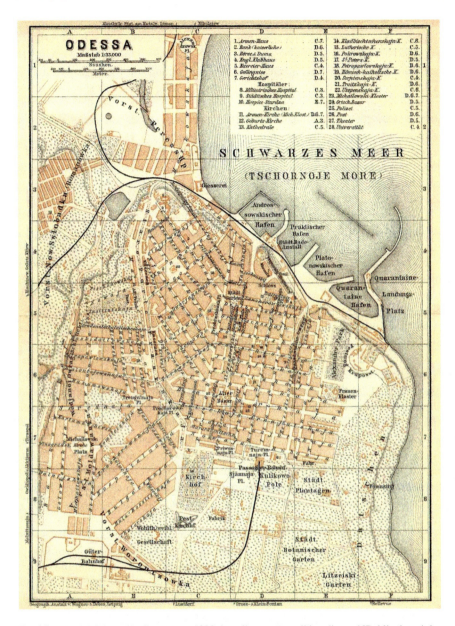

Fig. 4.3 Map of Odessa, in German, at 1892. http://commons.wikimedia.org/ [Public domain]

more Russian than its context, rather than more cosmopolitan. The cosmopolitanism became a memory, one to be proud of, but uneasily combined with the Russian emphasis of historical narratives. As in Trieste, the nationality question became dramatically simplified, this time to a Russian/Ukrainian distinction, with an additional

Jewish factor. For Jewish people, Odessa was not always paradise, and the shifting relations with western powers and westernizing influences also affected the position of the Jewish people, while the general economic and political situation had an influence, with pressure on Russia often translated in pressure on its minorities. Tanya Richardson describes beautifully how this history fraught with tensions becomes visible in discursive ruptures in history books, in stories, in heritage policies, in the selective renovation of buildings, and in the contrasting stories told about all this in heritage tours and within the remaining Jewish areas themselves (2005, 2008).

With the instability of the late empire, and later the Revolution and its aftermath, Odessa maintained a cosmopolitan air, but besides Russians and Ukrainians, virtually only Jewish people were left. Trade networks unravelled, just as with Trieste had been the case. What came back after the Russian revolution were links with other Soviet Republics, and the classical, European, southern images persisted, but without the networks to support them, to infuse them with new versions and images of 'Europe', antiquity and the south, to reinforce them with circulating products, people, ideas and fashions. Classical antiquity became its Soviet version, southern tourism became a Soviet tourism of collectives, spa's, stuffy museums, reused or dilapidated churches, canteen food and cheap wine and vodka (and great parties, it seems). After 2000, many buildings were renovated, painted, Ukrainian and Russian tourism came back, but with the recent turmoil over Crimea and in Eastern Ukraine, Odessa questioned its belonging to Ukraine again and poured over its history once more (Fig. 4.4).

What to say about Odessa cosmopolitanism? What was Odessa, in its most connected phase, the early 19th century, representative of, participating in, heading towards as first? Odessa was part initially of a Europeanizing Russia, and a Russia with an aspirational Mediterranean identity. The actual Mediterranean was never reached, and the Black Sea was the substitute. It had a mild climate and shared in a Greek, Roman, Byzantine heritage with the mediterranean (and Europe at large). Russia could be more European than western Europe, because its new southern roots, which were not seen as a conquest but a legitimate reconquest. Moscow was the legitimate successor of Constantinople (and Rome), so go south. Yet Russia wanted to be European but then not, was accepted but then not, was economically successful, and then not anymore. After Napoleon and 1812, after the Crimean war of 1852–54, after the Bolshevik Revolution, and intermittently, 'Europe' was not an acceptable model to emulate, and European elements and aspects were suspicious, had to be transformed or rejected. Once Italians and French and the others were hard to spot, what was left was a Jewish significant minority with surviving networks. The import of ideas was on their shoulders, sometimes appreciated, sometimes flaming distrust. Maintaining cosmopolitanism was their work, the work of official history (memorializing it in a sanitized form) and of the remaining architecture, as visual reminder (Friedberg 1991).

Odessan cosmopolitanism could never omit Russia, and Russia's idea of a world order it wanted to fit into, was not so clear. Both the order and the fitting were unstable constructs, so any place within its borders, however privileged, would be subjected to the tensions caused by this instability (cf Humphrey and Skvirskaja 2012). Actual foreign investment, and actual participation of foreign elements (with more than one option) in the development of cosmopolitan city cultures, was

4.2 Odessa

Fig. 4.4 Vintage postcard featuring Richelieu Street in Odessa. http://commons.wikimedia.org/ [Public domain]

therefore necessarily limited, and cosmopolitanism destined to be mostly a matter of narratives contained in the Russian (Soviet) world. And it was limited to those groups who were worse off somewhere else, and/or who were trained in navigating the violent politics and business of ambiguous empires: Jews, and to a lesser extent Greeks and Armenians (Zipperstein 1982; Driessen 2005; Sifneos 2005).

An aspect of Odessa that helped, we believe, to sustain many people in Odessa, and its image and self-image of cosmopolitan place, was the *combination of center and periphery*. Even in the most self-contained phases of its history, Russia was not self-contained. It cherished and needed margins of liminality, margins where other identities could flourish, bring in other goods, ideas, practices, where other experiences remained possible, where one could assume another identity, for a while, escape from totalizing pressures, have fun, break a few rules. Russia tolerated these margins and Odessa was an important example, where surviving diversity and dissension, surviving stories and networks, allowed for small infringements on the fringe, for a place to let steam off, to experiment, to see how bad those bad things are, and sometimes to enjoy them (Richardson 2008; Briker 1994).

4.3 Tbilisi

Tbilisi is the capital of Georgia, currently a republic. Before that it was a Soviet republic, before that a part of the Russian Empire (since 1801), and before that a kingdom with a complex history of fragmentation and unification. Tbilisi was less oriented towards Europe than the other cities, but it played the role of the cosmopolitan place of the Caucasus for several centuries. Baku and Erevan are much more recent creations, mostly of the early 20th centuries, but Tbilisi was a cultural, economic and political hub since the early middle ages. In Georgia, Persia, the Byzantines, and later the Ottomans fought for dominance, while Georgian polities regained territory time after time, starting from Tbilisi (Suny 1994). The 12th and early 13th centuries of King David the Builder and Queen Tamara serve as reference for a truly Georgian high tide, an open city culture within a strong Georgian kingdom (Van Assche et al. 2009b; Rapp 1997). In later centuries, cultural complexities accumulated, accumulating traces of changing positions of Tbilisi in Georgia, changing relations between parts of Georgia (under different influence/rule), and of Georgia in the region.

Tbilisi was never simply a Georgian city. In Tbilisi, the aristocratic elite was Georgian, while much of the economic elite consisted of Armenians, and many other groups coexisted for centuries, since its establishment in the 5th century. Kurds, Azeri, Greeks, Persians, later Germans, settled in the city. The old Narikala fortress includes 9th century Persian parts, while down the hill an Armenian church, a Georgian one, a mosque and a remnant of a Zoroastrian cult site are in close proximity to the ancient sulphur baths, for everyone (Suny 1994). Georgians were both top and bottom of the pyramid, the kings and the peasants around the city. A Georgian nobility which was unusually large (ca 10 % of the population) resided in city and countryside, in the city side by side with the Armenian merchants. Only

4.3 Tbilisi

under the Soviets became Tbilisi a predominantly Georgian city, in the sense of a majority Georgian ethnic population (Salukvadze, in Van Assche et al. 2009b).

Tbilisi's location on a branch of the Silk Road played a major role in this hybrid history, as well as the efforts by Georgian kings to keep Tbilisi on that road, and keep the road in Tbilisi. A 'Tbilisian' culture has been invoked many times, as transcending ethnic distinctions, and as introducing new distinctions within ethnic groups—Tbilisi Armenians versus other Armenians, eg (Rayfield 2013; Van Assche et al. 2009b; Suny 1994). For Armenians, the loss of their kingdom in the 11th century to the Turks, and the loss of their major cities sparked an exodus and a diaspora still visible today. Within the region however, many moved to Tbilisi and joined the already established Armenians. Erevan, the current capital of Armenia was a small backwater in a remote corner of the Persian empire for centuries when Russia took over the area (1801), and made it into the capital of a small republic dubbed Armenia. The old homelands were never reconquered. Russian and later Soviet investment turned Erevan into a large city of a million inhabitants, but until the collapse of the USSR, for many Armenians Tbilisi was still the hub, the cultural capital, as it had been the economic capital from ca 1100 until the early 20th century. Very recently, after independence, many Armenians left, others stayed. Small pockets of long time resident Muslim groups still live in the city, as well as traces of many groups reminding of the densely networked Soviet Union. Tbilisi was 'the city' in Georgia and in the Caucasus (Suny 1994; Grant 2010) (Fig. 4.5).

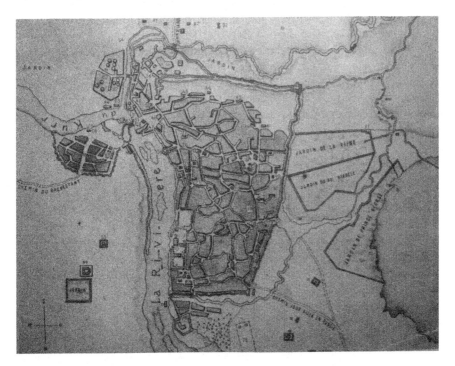

Fig. 4.5 Map of Tbilisi, drawn by the Russian officer Alexander Stepanovitch Pishchevich (1764–1820). http://commons.wikimedia.org/ [Public domain]

As with the other cities discussed, the cosmopolitan narratives have been reconstructed many times. In the case of Tbilisi, economic and cultural networks have shifted so many times that this had to have profound implications for the versions of cosmopolitanism experienced and cherished in the community. Different from Trieste and Odessa, Tbilisi was not so much an imperial creation. Indeed, much of what is currently old and of heritage value in the city, and its main urban structures, are 19th century Russian creations and recreations—with axes on two sides of the river, coming together in an older core reinvented after the last Persian invasion of 1796 (Van Assche and Salukvadze 2012). But it had existed centuries before, and it had developed its own cosmopolitanism slowly, independent of short term trade policies and economic booms (Suny 1994; Manning 2012). How to characterize Tbilisi cosmopolitanism, and distinguish it from Trieste and Odessa?

Tbilisi was not part of an empire that created it and then vanished itself. It was not part of an empire that pushed very hard for its creation and then got nervous. For much of its history, it was not connected to a very large political entity of which it had to be representative or for which it had to be a spearpoint in a desired direction of development and connectivity. It was also cosmopolitan at a smaller scale, so to say, a version less ambitious and less reflexive maybe, but more deeply engrained in city culture. Tbilisi never pretended to be the prime spot in the Russian Empire, or the most European or literally cosmopolitan place, but, because of its location, its rarity as a city, the dramatic events in the region, it became a community which was very distinct from its surroundings, and blending many elements of these surroundings in a Tbilisian culture. The food, music, dress, architecture, poetry, speech of many regions could be seen and heard and tasted, yet many elements also transformed into something local, representative of Tbilisi first of all (Van Assche et al. 2009b). Tbilisi was thus cosmopolitan because of its cultural layering, density, and transformative capacity. It did not come from representation or participation, not even in the old trade networks, since there were many places more prominent in them, and iconic because of that prominence (Bukhara, Khiva, Khokand, to name a few).

As in Trieste and Odessa, many people were multi-lingual, but this trait survived much longer, as it was not a rapid adaptation to a rapid assembly by higher powers, but a slow mutual adaptation of groups who did not easily consider moving out, who lived there because they considered it their natural place. The weaker tie with larger empires, when existing, also sheltered Tbilisi, its symbiosis, from disruptive tensions in and between empires (that is, from conflicting ambitions and identities spilling over internally). The 18th century poet and musician Sayyat Nova could switch effortlessly between Armenian, Georgian, Persian, in speech and in writing, and he was representative of a place marked by continuous code switching (Rayfield 2013). At the same time, the languages moved closer to each other in Tbilisi, borrowing words and expressions from each other. Certain art forms, songs, poetry, dance, cannot be understood as a sum of several elements with distinct ethnic origins, but a product of the Tbilisian city culture (Manning 2012) (Fig. 4.6).

4.3 Tbilisi

Fig. 4.6 The watermills on the flooded Mtkvari River, Tbilisi, in 1893 (photo taken by photographer Dimitri Ermakov). http://commons.wikimedia.org/ [Public domain]

In the 20th century, the Soviet regime brought in many Georgians from the regions to Tbilisi, to work in new industries, in government, at schools and universities. 'Old' Tbilisians complained, not that the place became Georgian, but that people brought their 'peasant mentality', i.e., in our view, an unfamiliarity with Tbilisian city culture, its mores and codes (Van Assche et al. 2009b). This was a complaint in early 20th century newspapers and magazines, and it is still heard now, a testament to the persistence of the Tbilisian blend, even after the disappearance of several of its original elements (Humphrey and Skvirskaja 2012).

4.4 Narratives and Networks and These Three

The previous sections already contained elements of comparison. We can say now that each city had a past more cosmopolitan than the present, that each city was a clear example of a local cosmopolitanism in the sense of a local city culture emerging as a result of larger networks, that at some point in the history, there was a growing awareness of difference with the environment, and similarity with a larger whole (cf Della Dora 2006; Driessen 2005). We can also say that the memories of that past have a variety of effects in the present. They inspire nostalgia for the past, for a more central position, but that nostalgia is easy, since history is more easily rewritten than remade. In each case, the networks supporting centrality, supporting a complex co-existence of many elements in the city, unraveled.

Tbilisi looks special because of the time it was granted to develop its cosmopolitanism, and, we believe, because of the absence of direct ties with higher centers of power who dreamed of and dictated a particular form of cosmopolitanism. It looks like the centralization of power that comes with an empire, and the resources this can mobilize to make a place cosmopolitan, comes at a price. Rapid development becomes possible, strong incentives to move, to live together, to identify with a place as the most modern, the most connected, the most varied. Yet the elements do not blend so quickly, and the demands can be high and volatile, especially in an active and ambitious empire. The larger whole to identify with is then, as said for Odessa, both the empire and the entity the empire is emulating or aspiring to be. Networks without an empire, without a clear and clearly higher center, can overlap empires, and can exist without empires. If they survive for a long time, they can create an environment for integration which can then transform the network; once nodes are formed, they can alter the flows in the networks.

Overlapping networks can more easily persist in the margin of empires, empires in the literal sense and empires metaphorically, as large centralized areas, with policies emanating from the center and visions for the development of the whole, and the desirable mixing of its elements (Shields 1994; Deleuze and Guattari 1987). Narratives of cosmopolitanism created by the center can linger on in the margin for a long time, and can be appropriated and transformed in the margin long after the center gave up. But such narratives can also emerge organically, that is, as a result of network dynamics, independent of other centers. The whole to identify with tends to be less articulated in such cases, as in Tbilisi, but one can find it nevertheless, in the distinction with the local, in the complexity of the blending, in the sense of overview of a large area, in geographical, cultural/ethnic and cognitive sense. Cosmopolitanism is a feature of a rhizomatic world, in places where more connections appear, and where somehow positive feed-back loops occur, with connections bringing in new connections, people bringing people bringing ideas bringing goods bringing memories of places and other people and goods and music (Driessen 2005; Sifneos 2005). This is apparently possible in both molar and nomadic polities (Deleuze and Guattari 1987).

The positive feedback loops in a rhizomatic environment can also more simply be described as creativity in and through diversity. We come close to the traditional analysis of creative cities, creative classes, and of urban superiority in the creation and maintenance of modern life (in the spirit of Richard Florida). In some ways, smaller cities now are as cosmopolitan as larger cities centuries back, more diverse in people, points of view, cultural and economic capital. This can be argued. What we are more interested in, however, is the combination of narrative and network, the explicit reference to difference from the environment, to a larger whole. And we are interested in reflexivity, in the use of these references to reflect on past and present, and, finally, to coordinate action and decision-making.

Cosmopolitanism, we believe, is a virtuality with strong performativity, strong reality effects (Van Assche et al. 2014), but also the potential to lead communities on traumatic paths, when the reality of old networks is forgotten in new or surviving narratives (Van Assche et al. 2009a).

Jacques Lacan can assist us. From Lacan, we borrow the triad of the Imaginary, the Symbolic and the Real, with a further distinction between the Imaginary Real, the Symbolic Real and the Real Real (Zizek 2008). Lacan does not use Deleuzian words, but also for him, memories can create realities, objects can create their own signs, and futures can reshape presents. All the modes of linkage in a rhizome were thinkable for Lacan. The symbolic order with him is the order of the sign, the world as a map of concepts distinguished from other concepts and linked to signs referring to them. That order breaks down sometimes, and is shaped elsewhere, by the forces of the Imaginary and the Real. Imaginaries are not images, narrative constructs, since these belong mostly to the Symbolic order. Imaginaries are constructive and disruptive, as they come from imaginary identifications, inextricably linked to old and largely unconscious desires, to examples and models we are not aware of, fear and avoidances we barely understand. The Real is then what can disrupt and construct the two others. It is not merely the physical world disrupting the symbolic signs assigned to them, the unexpected events, objects piercing through the fabric of signification, but just as well the unexpected feelings, anxieties, attachments, that re-signify ourselves and the world, including the constructs of the Imaginary. The Real is thus present and influential in all three domains, in a positive and negative way, and the same holds true for the Symbolic (since we cannot do anything without signification) and the Imaginary (since we are always a product of our early identifications).

Narrative and network, in our view, relate to each other as the Symbolic and the Real, while cosmopolitanism in its effects on identification and in the end policy, are largely the domain of the Imaginary. What disrupts cosmopolitan consciously constructed discourse is both the Real and the Imaginary. What makes many cosmopolitan dreams fall apart, is the lack of understanding of networks, as significant aspect of the Real, and the lack of reflexivity which can partly elucidate the pattern of identifications, and thus open more pathways to different futures.

In the next chapters, we will explore this terrain further, through the analysis of the past and present of Sulina, a small town in the Romanian Danube Delta, with a cosmopolitan past and a very modest present. Sulina can help us to getter a better grasp on the theme of virtuality and actuality in cosmopolitanism, on the relations between narratives and networks, and finally, it can further elucidate the fine mechanics of the local construction of cosmopolitanism. Trieste, Tbilisi and Odessa provided fine examples of local cosmopolitanism as the creation of city cultures emerging from special positions in networks and empires, sometimes dreaming of a new world order, sometimes more modestly seeing itself as a special, richer, place, a room with a view and an understanding to appreciate the view. What needs further investigation is the linkages between past, present and future as transformed through the lens of cosmopolitan narratives, in local discourse and action.

References

Bal M (2002) Traveling concepts. Yale University Press, New Haven
Ballinger P (2003) Imperial nostalgia: mythologizing Habsburg Trieste. J Mod Ital Stud 8(1):84–101
Briker B (1994) The underworld of Benia Krik and I. Babel's "Odessa stories". Can Slavonic Pap (Revue Canadienne des Slavistes) 115–134
Czaplicka J, Gelazis NM, Ruble BA (2009) Cities after the fall of communism: reshaping cultural landscapes and European identity. Johns Hopkins University Press, Baltimore
Delanty G (2009) The cosmopolitan imagination. The renewal of critical social theory. Cambridge University Press, Cambridge
Deleuze G, Guattari F (1987) A thousand plateaus. University of Minnesota Press, Minneapolis
Della Dora V (2006) The rhetoric of nostalgia: postcolonial Alexandria between uncanny memories and global geographies. Cult Geogr 13(2):207–238
Driessen H (2005) Mediterranean port cities: cosmopolitanism reconsidered. Hist Anthropol 16(1):129–141
Friedberg M (1991) How things were done in Odessa: cultural and intellectual pursuits in a Soviet City. Westview Press, Boulder
Fuchs S (2001) Against essentialism. Harvard University Press, Cambridge
Grant B (2010) Cosmopolitan Baku. Ethnos 75(2):123–147
Hinchman LP, Hinchman SK (eds) (1997) Memory, identity, community: the idea of narrative in the human sciences. SUNY Press, New York
Humphrey C, Skvirskaja V (eds) (2012) Post-cosmopolitan cities: explorations of urban coexistence. Berghahn Books, Oxford
Irwin-Zarecka I (1994) Frames of remembrance: the dynamics of collective memory. Transaction Books, New Brunswick
Legg S (2004) Memory and nostalgia. Cult Geogr 11(1):99–107
Luhmann N (1995) Social systems. Stanford University Press, Stanford
Magris C (2011) Danube. Random House, New York
Manning P (2012) Semiotics of drink and drinking. Bloomsbury, London
Massey D (2005) For space. Sage, London
Mills A (2006) Boundaries of the nation in the space of the urban: landscape and social memory in Istanbul. Cult Geogr 13(3):367–394
Minca C (2009) 'Trieste Nazione' and its geographies of absence. Soc Cult Geogr 10(3):257–277
Morris J (2002) Trieste and the meaning of nowhere. Da Capo Press, Boston
Rapp SH (1997) Imagining history at the crossroads: Persia, Byzantium, and the architects of the written Georgian past. University of Michigan, Ann Arbor
Rayfield D (2013) The literature of Georgia: a history. Routledge, London
Richardson T (2008) Kaleidoscopic Odessa: history and place in contemporary Ukraine, vol 35. University of Toronto Press, Toronto
Richardson T (2005) Walking streets, talking history: the making of Odessa. Ethnology 13–33
Shields R (1994) Places on the margin. Sage, London
Sifneos E (2005) "Cosmopolitanism" as a feature of the greek commercial diaspora. Hist Anthropol 16(1):97–111
Somers MR (1994) The narrative constitution of identity: a relational and network approach. Theory soc 23(5):605–649
Subtelny O (2009) Ukraine: a history. University of Toronto Press, Toronto
Suny RG (1994) The making of the Georgian nation. Indiana University Press, Bloomington
Thrift N (2005) Knowing capitalism. Sage, London
Van Assche K (2004) Signs in time. An interpretive account of urban planning and design, the people and their histories. Wageningen University, Wageningen
Van Assche K, Salukvadze J (2012) Tbilisi reinvented: planning, development and the unfinished project of democracy in Georgia. Plann Perspect 27(1):1–24

References

Van Assche K, Devlieger P, Teampău P, Verschraegen G (2009a) Forgetting and remembering in the margins: constructing past and future in the Romanian Danube Delta. Mem Stud 2(2):211–234

Van Assche K, Salukvadze J, Shavisvili N (eds) (2009b) City culture and city planning in Tbilisi. Where east and west meet. Mellen Press, Lewiston

Van Assche K, Beunen R, Duineveld M (2012) Performing success and failure in governance: Dutch planning experiences. Public Adm 90(3):567–581

Van Assche K, Beunen R, Duineveld M (2014) Evolutionary governance theory: an introduction. Springer, Heidelberg

Waley P (2009) Introducing Trieste: a cosmopolitan city? Soc Cult Geogr 10(3):243–256

Zipperstein SJ (1982) Jewish enlightenment in Odessa: cultural characteristics, 1794–1871. Jewish Soc Stud 19–36

Zizek S (2008) In defense of lost causes. Verso, London

Part III
The Small Worlds of Cosmopolitanism: Sulina

Chapter 5
Introduction: Sulina as Center and Margin

Abstract In this chapter, we analyze the town of Sulina as a place and a community marked by a history of marginality and centrality. We investigate how this duality and drama affects the way the place relates to the world at large, and sketch the geographical, historical and institutional context for our further investigations. We highlight the importance of the CED, the European Danube Commission, in reshaping Sulina in the past, in changing its image and self-image, and creating a path of remembering a planning which can still be detected.

Keywords Sulina · Social memory · European Danube Commission · Marginality · Network · Narrative · Politics · Crimean War

Sulina is a special place, a small town on the mouth of the Danube. It had an international importance in the late 19th and early 20th centuries, when it was the seat of the CED, the European Danube Commission, a forerunner of the EU that was established by the major European powers specifically to guard the mouth of the Danube, to put it under international control as a way to safeguard trade and to stabilize the border zone between the Russian and Ottoman Empires. This we know. In the early years of the CED, Romania did not exist as a nation state; later it did, but it did not control Sulina and the lower Danube, so it behaved as a competitor politically and economically.

Romania itself owes its independence to the same tensions that created Sulina and the CED: Russia was about to conquer the whole region, but this was not accepted by Europe, as too much upsetting the balance of power. Instead, Russia supported independence for Romania and Bulgaria, thus at least undermining the Ottomans and hopefully creating future allies or vassal states. That did not happen in the end. In 1878, when Romania became a state, it was much smaller than its present embodiment, did not include yet Transsylvania (Habsburg still), nor the lower Danube (CED rule) nor the Dobrogea (Bulgaria). When Dobrogea became part of Romania, the inhabitants were mostly not Romanian, and the mix of ethnicities on the coast results from a layered history dating back to the early

Greek colonies (7th cent. BC), and earlier. The western Black Sea coast was itself a cosmopolitan area, although impoverished in its connectivity in the unstable late Ottoman years. Romania felt unease and Dobrogeans were treated as second class citizens, with less rights than the people from the other regions. Between 1878 and 1913, Northern Dobrogea was subject to a *separate, extra-constitutional admini strative organization*, meaning that the inhabitants were denied political participation and the right to acquire properties outside the province. Dobrogea became "a melting pot of regional differences and a laboratory for fostering Romanian national identity" (Iordachi 2001: 135). Due to its multicultural character, Dobrogea, an important economical asset, was indeed a tough challenge for the young Romanian state, interested in homogenization and in building a coherent, strong national identity.

The new Romanian identity still had to crystallize, its history had to be written and taught, and the ethnic mix on the coast, with networks in all directions, did not fit the mold of the narratives Romania was crafting. Part of the newly born Romanian kingdom since 1878, Dobrogea was the subject of what Constantin Iordachi called "internal colonization": "its organization was characterized by administrative distinctiveness and excessive centralization supported by claims of cultural superiority of the core region, by intense ethnic colonization, and by uneven regional economic development tailored to the needs of the metropolis" (Iordachi 2001: 121–2). For this end, the Romanian political authorities employed a "threefold mechanism composed of ethnic colonization, cultural homogenization, and economic modernization. The most important stimulus behind the annexation of Dobrogea was economic: due to its strategic geographical location, the province was regarded as a vital commercial outlet of Romania, granting it access to the sea and facilitating thus its elevation into the world economy, from periphery to semi-periphery. Demographically, Northern Dobrogea served as an "Internal America" for Romania, a dynamic frontier zone of new settlements for expanding the national economy and ethnic boundaries" (Iordachi 2001: 122).

Right next door, the lower Danube was even longer inaccessible for Romania, up to the eve of the Second World War. Romania later co-decided, but was competing with the CED and favored Constanta as its own port, aided by the construction of a canal, rendering the Danube Delta less attractive for shipping. The international enterprise to stabilize the area by developing it, by controlling but also favoring trade, lost traction. Whereas the CED developed Sulina systematically, and attracted various groups to be active in trade and commerce, the tension with Romania later, the canal bypassing the Delta, the wars, and the marginalization of the area once Romania controlled it, did not help (Iordachi 2002). The hardening of the border with the USSR disrupted regional networks while the international networks had been unraveling for a while. Greeks, Armenians and Jewish largely disappeared, with the reduced opportunities that came with fragmenting networks, and the Western European bureaucratic elite disappeared immediately when the CED left. Other people came in, from the villages in the surrounding marshes, and kept the cosmopolitan memories alive (Fig. 5.1).

5 Introduction: Sulina as Center and Margin

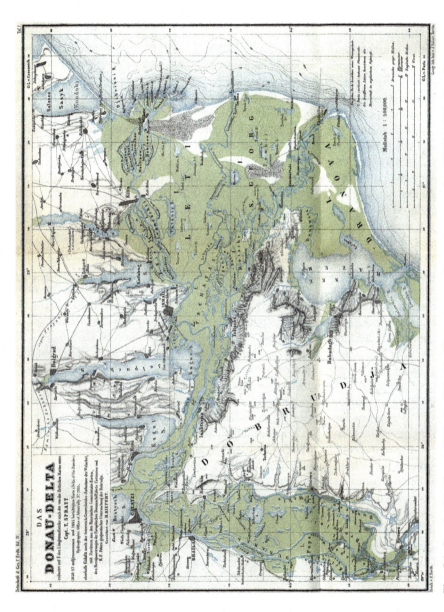

Fig. 5.1 Danube Mouths at 1867, by Heinrich Kiepert, geographer and cartographer (1818–1899). http://commons.wikimedia.org/ [Public domain]

In physical terms, the CED changed much of the landscape. Whereas older maps and drawings show a small fishing village with mostly Turkish architecture, and whereas old stories depict the place as a pirate's nest, new expertise and new rules came with the CED establishment. The British engineer sir Charles Augustus Hartley spent years studying the river system and embarked upon a large scale engineering program, including the straightening of the Sulina branch, the building of jetties into the Black Sea, to prevent the silting up of the mouth. Dredging operations took place, and of special importance was the clearing of sandbars in front of the mouth. These hindered navigation, causing ships to wait often for weeks before they could move up river, and they made ships an easy target for pirates.

Besides its duty regarding the amelioration of navigation on Danube, rendering the Sulina channel safe and sailable, the Commission was actively involved in the life of the community. In a kind of beneficial colonization, CED has built a hospital (1867–1869), the water castle (1903), the CED palace (1868), a telegraphic line linking Sulina to Tulcea and Galati (1857) and a telephonic line since 1903, has organized the cemetery (1864—the Christian one, 1871—the Muslim one), has introduced public illumination with petroleum (electricity since 1910). Also, CED had a very active role in sponsoring all religious confessions, contributing to a milieu of multicultural tolerance (1865—the Catholic Church, 1866—the Russian orthodox, 1869—protestant and Greek orthodoxe, 1870—a mosque). At the beginning of the XX century, there were two Romanian schools, two Greek, one German, one Jewish and French pension. On the beach there was a Casino; the city had many restaurants, a theater, a typography and newspapers. By 1930, CED had 359 employees (208 Romanians), adding 746 temporary workers (567 Romanians), all generously paid in golden francs (Teampău and Van Assche 2007: 265–6).

Western European architects and engineers were engaged in the expansion of the city on an elongated grid pattern (Rosetti et al. 2006, 25), with streets numbered instead of named, the American way. Areas were drained, the Sulina branch of the Danube canalized, levies built, a graveyard laid out on an island (Micu and Bucur 2006). Besides its duty regarding the amelioration of navigation on Danube, rendering the Sulina channel safe and sailable, the Commission was actively involved in the life of the community. In a kind of beneficial colonization, CED has built a hospital (1867–1869), the water castle (1903), the CED palace (1868), a telegraphic line linking Sulina to Tulcea and Galati (1857) and a telephonic line since 1903, has organized the cemetery (1864—the Christian one, 1871—the Muslim one), has introduced street lighting with petroleum (electricity since 1910). Also, the CED had a very active role in sponsoring all religious confessions, contributing to a milieu of multicultural tolerance (1865—the Catholic Church, 1866—the Russian orthodoxe, 1869—protestant and Greek orthodoxe, 1870—a mosque; See Micu and Bucur 2006; Tatu 2005; Rosetti et al. 2006; Van Assche et al. 2009: 215) (Fig. 5.2).

Education in Sulina was at a high level, mostly organized along ethnic lines. Cultural and intellectual life flourished in the various communities, and Sulina was a well-known place all over Europe, a place frequently mentioned in the newspapers, a place of a cosmopolitan modernity. At the beginning of the 20th century, there were two Romanian schools, two Greek, one German, one Jewish and French boarding school. "If you were lucky as a Romanian, you got into a foreign

Fig. 5.2 Birdseye view of the Sulina Mouth of the Danube, showing the works of improvement carried out under the European Commission of the Danube, by Charles A. Hartley, Engineer in chief to the commission (first published in *The Illustrated London News*, 19 October 1861). http://commons.wikimedia.org/ [Public domain]

school, and then the world opened up" said one informant, later adding (with obvious embellishment) "many people spoke 4–5 languages in those days". On the beach there was a Casino; the city had many restaurants, a theater, a typography and newspapers. By 1930, CED had 359 employees (208 Romanians), adding 746 temporary workers (567 Romanians), all generously paid in golden francs (Micu and Bucur 2006, 46). All this incredible progress was cut short with World War One, during which Sulina was literally turned to ruins. But after 1920, the city is reconstructed, with more schooling institutions (teaching languages: Romanian, French, Italian, English, Russian), and in 1932 Sulina becomes a fashionable resort for thousands of tourists (Panighiant 1972, 9; Van Assche et al. 2009: 215–6).

Right before CED, Sulina was making headlines in 1854, after the place was literally turn ed into ashes by the British ship *Spitfire* in response to the killing of Admiral Parker's son by the locals. "Sulina is at present desolation personified" wrote *The Illustrated London News* on 2 September 1854. "Dogs and cats, of every grade of leanness, are the permanent occupants of the place. […] Lower down, a meagre supply of trees rises occasionally from the low swampy shore. […] The whole of the inhabitants of Sulina have retreated to Tultcha. There is no doubt but that they are a set of marauding ruffians, and practise all kinds of extortions on the many ships that pass out the Sulina mouth, through the year. Before taking their final departure, they went on board a Dutch galliot, lying quietly in the river, and plundered her of everything. These fellows are Greeks, of the Ionian and Albanian class". By the end of 1856, Sulina reportedly had between 2000 and 5000 inhabitants, dealing with navigation for some time of the year and engaging in heavy drinking for the rest (Tatu 2005: 287).

Some six decades later, we can read on a postcard from 1913 that somebody was visiting Sulina "a beautiful city, in the true meaning of the word—different world, different life". In between this two historical moments, form the gloomy days of the mid-XIX century uncertain political times to the prosperity of an attractive harbor, Sulina became the cosmopolitan city with a rich life.

With the CED, the pirates and the sandbars disappeared, as well as the Turkish architecture. Sulina was rebuilt on a grid pattern, with numbered streets, starting from the harbor (1st street) to the areas in the back of its narrow land base, where the sand gave away to the salt marshes. The first few streets were the most prestigious ones, where the western European bureaucrats lived and the Greek, Jewish and Armenian traders. There, one can find neo-classical mansions in rich ornament, whereas further back the dwellings are smaller, more organized around small courtyards, and on the edges and the margins, one could find the Russian and Ukrainian speaking fishermen.

These fishermen gradually became more prominent, as the international networks disappeared, largely after World War II. A simultaneous Russification and Romanization took place, in the sense that other languages disappeared, that people from the villages moved in, and that the Romanian state took control of administration and education. Previously, the CED had fostered consciously a multi-cultural community, with schools for the different ethnic groups, a multi-lingual administration (though dominated by French), and an array of events to emphasize unity in diversity. The communists, after the war, brought in different groups, from different regions, to work in new factories (fish canning) and in agriculture and pisciculture, but they were assimilated into the generic Romanian label relatively fast.

After the Second World War, Sulina and the broader Danube region became marginalized, with the unraveling of networks of places, people, information and the flow of goods (cf Smith 1998). 'The Armenians even took their tombstones with them', is an often repeated chant regarding marginalization (simultaneously a veiling of a tragic history). 'All the Greeks who could leave, left, many of them to the old motherland', is another recurring motif. Whatever was once cosmopolitan and 'European' in Sulina has long been drummed out by the Second World War and the subsequent communist rule. Once an important node in the borderlands connecting Europe and the Ottoman-dominated Black Sea area, time and circumstances have shifted it to the European periphery.

While northern Dobrogea can be described as an internal frontier, spearpoint of development in the late 19th and early 20th century for Romania, and while Sulina on the edge of the Delta, received its temporary centrality from the CED and collaborating minorities, the Delta-marshes themselves, can only be described as utterly marginal. Most people in Tulcea, on the western edge of the Delta, would consider Sulina a part of the Delta, but for many locals in Sulina, this amounts to an insult. Sulina is a free port; it belongs to the Sea and to the Danube, not to the swamp that surrounds it on three sides (for instance, the inhabitants from outside Sulina are called in contempt *băltăreți*, i.e. "people from the swamp"). It belongs to the fostered and revitalized image of the European Sulina, not to the land of impoverished, barely literate and rather aggressive fishermen—as the Delta is often depicted in opposition to the cosmopolitan and highly educated city environment. Newcomers have become assimilated into the preexisting social memories, and the topography of memory rejuvenates the European narrative. Interestingly enough, the image of the Delta region as one vast marginal area, far from the centres of power, their regulative controls and value systems, is closely related to another narrative of self produced in Sulina: the pirates' nest. Region and city are opposed on one level, and merge into one big narrative of proud marginality and defiance of authority on another.

In this environment, local cosmopolitanism existed under centrality and it exists under marginality. In the following chapters, we discuss different mechanisms appertaining to local cosmopolitanism through the lens of a series of concepts: narrative, identity, migration, performance, marginality, memory, boundary, palimpsest and policy. After these micro-analyses, we attempt to bring together the diverging story-lines again in a second synthetic view of local cosmopolitanism.

References

Iordachi C (2001) The California of the Romanians: the integration of Northern Dobrogea into Romania, 1878–1913. In: Trencsényi B (ed) Nation-building and contested identities: Romanian and hungarian case studies. Regio Books, Budapest, pp 121–152

Iordachi C (2002) Citizenship, nation-and state-building: the integration of Northern Dobrogea into Romania, 1878–1913. The Carl Beck Pap Russ East Eur Stud 1607:86

Micu C, Bucur S (eds) (2006) Sulina—European destiny: the 150th anniversary of the European Commission of the Danube. Tulcea County Council and Sulina City Hall, Tulcea

Panighianț E (1972) Le delta du Danube. Edition Touristique

Rosetti C et al (2006[1931]) La commission Europeenne du Danube et son oeuvre, de 1856–1931. Imprimerie Nationale, Paris

Smith G (ed) (1998) Nation-building in the post-soviet borderlands: the politics of national identities. Cambridge University Press, Cambridge

Tatu T (2005) Cărți vechi, corăbii, reisi, neguțători și diplomați, Dunărea de Jos, 1745–1856 (Old maps, documents and treaties regarding the lower Danube). Editura Istru, Bucharest

Teampău P, Van Assche K (2007) Sulina, the dying city in a vital region: social memory and nostalgia for the European future. Ethnologia Balkanica 11(1):257–278

Van Assche K, Devlieger P, Teampău P, Verschraegen G (2009) Forgetting and remembering in the margins: constructing past and future in the Romanian Danube Delta. Memory Studies 2(2):211–234

Chapter 6
Narratives of Place and Self

Abstract In this chapter, we discuss several narrative dynamics central to the functioning of local cosmopolitanism. We look at the interplay between biographical, autobiographical and place narratives, at the role of consistency and inconsistency in them, and connect this with a reflection on the functioning of social memory. We show that memory needs reproduction, selection, relies on gatekeepers and promoters, and can be instrumentalized within limits. Then we move to a reflection on marginality in Sulina and more broadly the Danube delta, its different meanings and aspects, and its different effects on remembering, on identity construction, and on emerging forms of cosmopolitanism. Shifting boundaries, in spatial, social and conceptual sense, represent both obstacles and enablers in the functioning of local cosmopolitanism, in its local transformations.

Keywords Place · Narrative · Community · Identity · Memory · Marginality · Biography · Autobiography · Landscape · Gatekeepers of memory · Borders · Boundaries

6.1 Autobiography, Biography, and Place

People tell stories about themselves, others and the place they live in, and the entwining of these stories creates the frame for identity construction. In this chapter, we focus on the way narratives of self and others are entwined, but without overemphasizing their cohesion. Sulina demonstrates how stories of self, others and place can compete against each other, within one category of narratives and between the categories. Just as individual identity is a narrative construct with an elusive core and questionable cohesion, and just as this allows the individual to adapt the changing circumstances in her life, narratives of social identity do not provide a unifying frame defining the community. The polyvocality of the community does not only represent a natural multiplicity because community is not entirely pre-given; it also represents an array of adaptation strategies to shifting internal and external circumstances. (The community, however, *is* pre-given in the sense that community narratives and networks exist before the individual, they can also adopt new groups into places with old stories).

Stories people tell about places serve not only to position them in a desired location, but also to delineate social boundaries, to assert who "belongs" and who doesn't, to clarify *who we are* (Bird 2002). In other words, "narratives make places habitable and believable, […] they organize the invisible meanings of the city" (Simonsen 2008: 146). If we look at the discursive makeup of landscape, we can notice that contesting meanings of urban belonging and divergent stories and memories are crucial for the local identity and for articulating the future of the city. Since every city is a privileged space of diversity and heterogeneity, "collective memory" is just a rhetorical construction, while in fact "there is a plurality of social memories in every city—each particular to a different group and routed in the material and mental spaces it has experienced" (Bélanger 2000: 78). As Fiona Allon argues, in such encounters, "the city is produced as a distinctive and marketable place with a particular myth of identity at the same time as it is being rewritten by global economic forces operating above and beyond its boundaries" (Allon 2004: 55).

Sulina is a special place, as the stories being told about it can hardly find an anchor in the present day urban landscape. While history visibly lingers in the decayed walls of old houses, we are not presented with information about those buildings, but rather an abstract narrative of a once prosperous city that does not need "proofs" or material remains to hold true. A local museum in a former lighthouse is primarily focused on the local hero and writer Jean Bart and the activities of CED, but does not portray the multicultural life of the prewar city. Neither, would we argue, does the annual Festival of Minorities which attempts to showcase the ethnic diversity of the region (Greeks, Lipoveni, Turks, Tatars, Armenians etc.), but in fact preserves a visible "propaganda" overtone, nor the widely advertised "maritime cemetery" with its separate sections for Christians, Jewish, Muslim and Lipoveni old-believers. All these mnemonic places seem to be isolated items in the complex web of local history. There are almost no narrative links between the existence of this unique cemetery and the peculiar urban life of multicultural Sulina that enabled it, besides the names of the characters present in the stories.

As Greeks, Armenians, Jews and western Europeans moved out, connections were lost. We have argued elsewhere that "through the Jewish, Armenian and Greek communities, and through the institution of the CED, Sulina was embedded in the wider world, and that world could leave its imprint locally. The marginalization caused a loss of memory. 'People in Sulina knew what was going on in Paris', locals told us, and one can add that Parisian readers were also familiar with Sulina, seat of a significant international organization (the francophone CED). The CED itself was part of a pan-European network—and indeed was one of the first pan-European networks itself. The merchant minorities attracted by CED investment, free trade and favorable geopolitics had little business in Sulina after the disappearance of the CED and changing geopolitics. With that, their schools, cultural

6.1 Autobiography, Biography, and Place

organizations, churches, local and foreign newspapers, artefacts, skills, interactions with others, etc. disappeared. Western and eastern networks once converging in Sulina fragmented as power and trade shifted (see Albert et al. 2001; Judt 2007; Magris 1988[1986]; Rosetti et al. 2006[1931]; Van Houtum and Van Naerssen 2002; Van Assche et al. 2009: 217–218).

Nowadays, very few people have actual memories of the life in the Sulina of the CED. They and others gloss over the problems of the place, the sometimes restrictive ethnic boundaries (Ukrainians and Lipoveni working in the homes of Greeks and Armenians), and imagine it as place without boundaries, without conflict (Anderson 1982). A place where all the goods and the good things of the world came together. Reflections on the artificial character of its centrality are rare, and so are potential critics. "In this new image, the contingent, fragile, artificial character of Sulina's temporary centrality under the CED (Iordachi 2002; Teampău and Van Assche 2007a, b) is never considered, nor the reasons for its temporary success and its downfall. The policy frame that created the CED is not observed, the western and oriental networks that allowed for its prospering not part of the narrative. One forgets everything it took to turn Sulina into an exception, forgets the loss of infrastructure, of networks. 'The Europeans' (not specifically the CED) came, poured money in and were drawn to the tax-free zone, is a commonly held belief: 'they brought lots of gold'; 'if we could just have a free port again, less taxes'." (Van Assche et al. 2009: 224).

The history of Sulina and the wider regions reveals a pervasive ambiguity and volatility in the construction of identities on these scales. During the Danube Commission era, Sulina was detached from its Delta context, and a new identity was rapidly constructed which turned the margin into a centre. Sulina acquired some central functions, attracted people and activities because of the CED, and the pivotal role it created for the town. In his well known novel "Europolis", the author, Jean Bart (former Commisioner and commander in chief of the Harbor at the beginning of the XIXth century) calls Sulina "a cosmopolite city—a mosaic of races at the mouth of the old river Danubius". He also acknowledges the functioning of CED, which he must have known directly, as „a small world in itself, Europe in miniature, with sceneries, backstages and protocole, that has a life of its own" (Bart 2004, first published 1933).

Truth be told, the Sulina of the CED—a product of a complex mixture of local, regional, international forces and people, of geopolitics embodied in village schools—was hard to understand for anyone. This complexity, we argue, the strong rhetoric of the CED itself, in addition to the present EU rhetoric, as well as the distance in time and absence of possibly opposing minority views, all contribute to the local dominance of the master narrative of an affluent, stable, tolerant, sophisticated European past and future. The master-narrative reshaped to a certain extent the ethnic identities locally, and this in turn shapes the negotiation between personal experience, personal narrative, and group narrative" (Teampău and Van Assche 2009a: 62).

After WWII, under the new communist rule, waves of peasants and people form the neighbouring villages were attracted to the city. At that time, the international networks of the CED period had disappeared, and Sulina lost its allure. One of the people who came to the city after the war recounts: "when I came to Sulina, in 1952, the city was old, old. It was very cold and the houses were old, empty and cold". Group memories either disappeared quickly, when people moved out suddenly, or faded slowly, as in the Greek case, because the people lost their connections with their international network, and left behind the production of knowledge, memory and identity: 'I think I have an uncle on one of the islands, I don't know if he's still alive.' Under communism, international connections were under suspicion, contact was limited and pressure to identify as Romanian high. A purely folklorist ethnic identity was allowed—'there are no ethnic problems, they all have their festivals'. And a Sulinese identity was forged, incorporating the reinterpreted memories of mostly disappeared communities (see also Van Assche et al. 2009: 218).

One can witness now in Sulina, on festive occasions, such as The Official Days of the City (August 15th each year, an event that we have observed for the past nine years), how "multiculturalism" is exhibited, mostly for the sake of tourists (that date is also the peak of the summer season) in the form of several dances and songs performed by Greek and Lipovan ensembles. There are already two dance groups at the Greek Community, composed of teenagers and young children, with colorful costumes and entertaining music; most of them, surprisingly or not, are Lipovan: there are not many Greeks left, and being part of the dance ensemble is very attractive, mostly for reasons of paid trips abroad and in the country, and summer camps in Greece. That explains why performing folk dances can be attractive for teenagers with cool T-shirts featuring rock bands. On the other hand, the lipovan culture is represented by two choirs, mainly composed of elderly people, few man and several old ladies, with their high-pitched voices and blue scarves. Behind the scenes, the head of the Lipovan Community, Mr. Halchin confessed to the difficulty of organising these chores. "They, the old ones, used to sing on the streets of their villages, but then it was forbidden during communism. And now, they still feel ashamed to sing in public. I could hardly convince them".

In Sulina, the local performance of multiculturalism is shaped by communist policies and practices and the 'Sulina' synthetic image, the local myth of cosmopolitanism. The catastrophic episodes of war and dismantling of CED allowed for the present function of the Sulina myth, since the systematic loss of connections with the CED past, its networks, its people, made it possible to alter the image of the CED era more freely. More recently, democratization, conversion to a market economy, the impact of tourism and European integration have further transformed the performance of multiculturalism. These processes are having an influence on images of place, self, and other invoked and marketed (Van Assche and Teampău 2009: 14).

The rupture caused by the disintegration of the CED and by the war, allowed for the appropriation and transformation of the CED myth first underground in postwar communist Sulina and then in the open after the end of socialism. With the end of communist rule, Romanians decided they wanted to be European again and join the European Union. The marginal city of Sulina represented an

6.1 Autobiography, Biography, and Place

opportunity to construct and market a European past as a key to the European future. Europe pushed actively for institutional reform, for the cultivation of democratic values including multiculturalism and the protection of the heritage of various communities. In Sulina, European grants and subsidies have been pursued by invoking a multicultural past and present that is based on a reified conception of cultural identity. The promotion of Sulina in the city and region consistently refers to the CED myth, and contemporary multiculturalism which is assumed to be similar to earlier forms. The city is presented as an example of modern European multiculturalism (see also Van Assche and Teampău 2009: 15).

We can say that the myth of CED Sulina feeds off the modern European mythologies (including their version of culture and multiculturalism) and vice versa. Both the localized myth of the past of Sulina and the myth of a European common destiny in diversity reinforce each other locally. The local palimpsest of multiculturalism is therefore connected not only to images of a cosmopolitan past, but also images of a cosmopolitan future. CED and EU are conflated, and the local and temporal features of cosmopolitanism forgotten.

In Sulina, we observed over and over again how people could tell stories about Sulina, positive and negative, only partially consistent, and then move to stories about the communities in Sulina, and stories about personal histories and family experiences recounted in small circles, which were even less consistent with the positive narratives about Sulina. This might not be surprising, as identities in particular and narratives more generally have various effects and a variety of uses, depending on circumstances, goals and audience. The positive narratives of 'Sulina', the appearance itself of 'Sulina' stories, invokes often the gloss and polish of the cosmopolitan CED era, which is supposed to represent the positive essence of Sulina, what it could be and what it was. It is the virtual positive of Sulina, for many of the storytellers. Whether the virtual can have real effects in this case, hinges on other factors. We can draw a parallel with the stories about the 'Danube Delta', the surrounding marshlands and in fact the region. Also this concept comes up as a master signifier of entwined discourses of nature conservation and resistance against it.

The success of other boundary-maintaining mechanisms such as the CED myth, can be partly attributed to residents' perception of isolation, neglect, and opaque, poorly enforced rules emanating from the center. The collective perception of being in the margin is fertile ground for the production of new signs of difference from the outside world as well as local unity. A similar attitude can also be observed in the dealings of local government in Sulina with the regional (and national) governments. City hall prefers to develop plans and policies with minimal communication with the other levels of government because these other levels cannot be trusted and it is better to rely on one self. Policies developed at other levels are rarely implemented in Sulina (Van Assche and Teampău 2009: 15).

Sulina also shows how people can craft new narratives of self that rely on social narratives to very different degrees. At one point, one can recount the story of glorious Sulina in its cosmopolitan days, and a bit later tragic memories of individual suffering and yet at a different moment glimpses come to the surface of older stories, heard from others, about the less attractive sides of old cosmopolitan Sulina, where some groups where clearly privileged and others worked for them. Each of these stories can have a personal component and a social component, and these cannot always be distinguished; each of them can be tinged to a different degree and in a different manner by the circulating narratives on place and community (Teampău and Van Assche 2009b).

They are likely not entirely compatible and this incompatibility is likely not observed or reflected upon. Freud already knew that the cohesion of personal and social identity is a productive myth, one enabling us to function, to organize and survive, to reduce complexity and to maintain morality. Cosmopolitanism can per definition only be a myth, since there are always various ways to observe and participate in larger networks, to interpret and navigate, but in the case of Sulina, the myth functions differently as there are in fact few traces of memory which can be traced back directly to the glorified period. And since there is a deep awareness of being not central, not cosmopolitan, reinforced by standard Romanian discourses about the Danube Delta and Sulina as 'the end of the world' (Teampău and Van Assche 2007a, b).

One cannot simply label one of them as the cosmopolitan narratives; in some cases this might be true, in many others there are shades of cosmopolitanism in the various narratives available to individual and community. Autobiography, biography, and narratives of place identity are not cohesive and also not nearly divided into categories with more or less cosmopolitan character. Person, group and place relate differently all the time, and the more mythical character of the cosmopolitan Sulina makes it easier to manipulate the stories, and to refashion personal identities (Van Assche and Teampău 2009). The ethnic labels do not always appear as important, and historical mixes of groups can be emphasized more on one moment, less a bit later. The movement of people out of Sulina, and the highly fluctuating 'value' or appreciation of certain identities or aspects of identity made categories even more fluid.

In the case of Sulina, new people came to the place after the international networks that gave rise to its cosmopolitan character unraveled; the newcomers were absorbed into the existing narratives, and these narratives were simultaneously transformed. Most of the current inhabitants come from the marshes surrounding the town (Van Assche et al. 2008; Van Assche and Teampău 2009). These marshes themselves were transformed, not only through nature conservation, but also through a hardening of the border with Ukraine, cutting through older networks in the Russian and Ukrainian speaking communities. In living memory, vegetables used to come from Vilkovo, across the border, fisherman moved back and forth, and commerce ignored the border. Unstable identities in fragmenting networks are the norm, not the exception, and the instability throws an important light on the normal processes of identity construction and reconstruction.

It seems that the official 'Sulina' narrative offers safe grounds to talk about multiculturalism. Belonging can be expressed and experienced through various senses. When experienced, it can be articulated or not. Sulina residents have many concerns; their ethnic belonging and interethnic encounters are not high on their agendas. This is partly the consequence of tragic histories some of which are remember and others of which are not. It is also the consequences of short-term thinking and short-term concerns in this harsh marginal environment (Van Assche et al. 2012) which means there is little place for excessive ethnic pride. It is also the result of a history of the mixing of identities through marriage, assimilation, forgetting, however the 'original' identities are conceived (see also Van Assche and Teampău 2009: 16).

After all, the very ethnic groups that made Sulina the "most cosmopolitan city in the country" are no longer there. The functioning of CED with its many representatives and employees of different ethnicities who worked together and communicated on a daily basis likely had an important role in generating the "cosmopolitan" outlook of the city. However, the French, the British, the Dutch, Italians, Germans etc. are not "remembered" by contemporary residents (except for few cases where the informants' family had personal connections to them). Ethnic groups that remained in the collective memory are people who were part of the multicultural day-to-day life of the city and involved in its social networks and in the fabric of urban co-existence: Jews, Armenians, Turks, and Greeks. Their involvement in trade and commerce had a significant influence on the built environment and forms of urban sociality in the city (Fig. 6.1).

Today, most of the inhabitants are either Romanians, or Lipoveni, who came to Sulina, "to the city", from neighboring villages. According to the last census, from a total population of 5140, 82.5 % are Romanians, 10.6 % Lipoveni, 2.14 % Ukrainians, 1.3 % Greeks, and 0.2 % Turks. Very few are old enough to actually remember Sulina before the war; some of them learn anew about Sulina's glorious past, and should be less likely to long for a past they have no connection to (biographical and/or affective). Nonetheless, as Pine, Kaneff and Haukanes have made clear, conflicts over memory are not only about the historical truth, but also about identity claims and power. In this case, divergence over memory can hide an underlying, tacit divergence between groups, who develop loyalties and memories of different times. After all, many of the Lipoveni and Romanians used to work for the Greeks and Armenians—main characters in the nostalgic narratives—sometimes as domestic servants. Even when they participate in a common mnemonic account of Sulina's "good times", details of their own biography locates them in different social strata and places.

After World War II, groups that had previously worked for the now-vanished urban elites (Greeks, Armenians, Jews) became the dominant groups in the city. Despite this, it is still possible to trace the embellishment of these narratives, some old tensions, and some counter-narratives. In longer interviews, Sulina's elderly residents refer to significant hardships, distrust, and class inequality partly tied to ethnic distinctions. Autobiographical narratives that do not hide the negative aspects of pre-war life of the place, dramatic family histories stretching back to the CED period, do clash frequently with the positive Sulina myth of prosperous, tolerant cosmopolitanism. The tensions between the rosy Sulina myth and more gritty stories are often not observed by the local story-tellers, switching effortlessly from one register to another. Anecdotes about the tragedies of the war reveal the quick dissolution of the social fabric of the CED period, a fabric that had been deteriorating before. As in many other places, the war brought simmering tensions,

Fig. 6.1 Ethnic map of Sulina area, according to the Romanian census of 1930. http://commons.wikimedia.org/ [Public domain]

envy, and distrust to the surface. The sheer quantity of stories about the riches of the urban elites, their fate, and the enduring suspicions among Sulinese regarding the appropriation of that old wealth betray, on the one hand, the power of the glorified CED-narrative, and on the other hand fissures in that narrative. Longer interviews reveal that few people had any problem with the departure of other ethnic groups. What happened to their assets was far more important. Few stories acknowledged the role of the networks and geopolitics of Western Europeans, Greeks, Armenians and Jews in the rise and functioning of Sulina.

Other narratives, less mainstream, describe the difficult life of a special category of colonists: peasants from Transylvania who came to Dobrogea pushed by the poverty and famine in their own homeland, or, after the Balkan wars, peasants who received land as reward for their military service (of course, behind this generous act was also the official policy of "Romanianizing" the region).

One old lady, descendant from a Transylvanian family that came to the delta to raise cattle has a version of the life in Sulina during CED which seems clearly less glamorous and desirable: *"Those who owned shops and taverns had a better life, but those who didn't, not so much. They were poor, very poor, and their daughters became servants in the houses of the former. Some people had beautiful houses, while others didn't even have a fence around their hut. Owners of shops and taverns were mostly Greeks and Jews; others worked in the port, to unload the ships, but that work was seasonal, and in between seasons, they were poor. Unless they had some kind of household, they would starve to death. Fishermen left home on Monday and came back on Saturday, and on Saturday they washed and went to the tavern. Monday morning they came out of the tavern and went back to the swamp. They didn't have any kind of furniture in the house, just a bed, made of four sticks in the ground, with a few planks and straw, if they had them, if not, just reed, and at night it made a lot of noise. Lots of people came here, peasants, shepherds form other parts of the country, hoping for a better life. Many of them had daughters, after the war there were few men left, and some of the luckiest of these girls married Greek men and became themselves Greek"* (Teampău 2013: 64–5). The last argument alludes to the desirability of some ethnic status that came also with desirable social and economic advantages: being Greek was better than others and it is still more glamorous today, as we will describe in the following chapters.

Lipoveni did not have an easy life, either, especially during CED, since most of them were either fishermen living in rather closed communities, or working in temporary, unskilled positions for CED. One elder man recalls his first years of school in Sulina, at the Romanian school: *"When we came here, there were many young ladies, with fancy dresses, daughters of rich businessmen or pilots of CED, and us, lipoveni we were wearing clothes made from our elder brothers' clothes and fishermen boots. But we were the best in math!"* (Teampău 2011: 72). Obviously, there were tensions and frustrations, and they are still visible in the identity discourse of Lipoveni. In the case of the respondent quoted above, he mentions quite often that "*lipoveni young men had to work hard to prove that they are reliable, responsible, good workers and good professionals*". Tensions were more intense right after WWII, when communists came to power (after 1947).

Many locals remember, but avoid stressing it, that for a while, in the '50s, lipoveni were privileged by the regime, due to the symbolic closeness to USSR and Russians. Several mayors of Sulina were lipovan, and most of them selected on ideological grounds. People "remember" lipovans saying in those times, with superiority: "the country is yours, the power is ours".

Of course, most of these details were conveniently forgotten, but do pop up in narratives when somebody's biography was directly influenced. In general, Lipoveni still have a bad reputation, of drunks, wife-beaters and lazy people, but most locals of Sulina would avoid stating these things outright. During the communist rule, however, many Lipoveni had a chance to improve their lives by becoming workers, moving to Sulina "to the city" and proving, once and again, that they are reliable and hard-working. The price they paid was not only leaving their native villages and families, but also leaving behind their traditions, way of life and language. "*A world was over, when that village disappeared. And now it's this new world, of Sulina*", says Mr. Halchin, talking nostalgically about his native village, Sfistofca. He remembers that up until the early '60s the village was still full of life, but then from 1965 especially young people started to leave massively to find work in the city "*and suddenly the village was left empty*". Nowadays the exodus continues: "*well, the children of those who left in the '60s–'70s now leave from Sulina, because they were born here; they leave to Tulcea, Constanta, Galati, Bucuresti, and after the revolution, abroad*" (Teampău 2011: 77).

As head of the Lipovan Organization in Sulina, mr. Halchin did his best to revive the sense of community among his co-ethnics. However, many of them, once they settled in Sulina, chose to give up completely their old label. He describes it as a sad situation: "*In fact, ethnicity is not important, just like it is not important if you were born on a Monday or Thursday; unless it was important since childhood. But still, identity is important, but it is up to the individual if it will be performed or not. Unfortunately, many people give it up without even knowing what they give up. Many of them say: I am not a lipovan, just live me alone! But I know he is, and that is so bad, actually, not bad, but rather sad to think that somebody is ashamed or afraid to be who they are. If his parents are lipoveni, and we know them, and they are from our village, how can one say that he is not lipovan? There's no way you are not, because you are!*" (Teampău 2011: 83–4). Another informant confirmed this idea: "*we all know each other here, we know each other's family and parents, so we know who we are, but some pretend to be Greek, especially by marriage, and we know she's Ukrainian, for instance*". Some of the ethnic trespassing is sanctioned by the community, some are not, and in many situations we have observed a kind of flexibility in terms of ethnic identification. Noticeably, the Greek identity is the most glamorous and desirable, and where possible (through marriage, or having one parent of Greek origin) people prefer to identify as Greek.

On the other hand, in traditional lipovan contexts, things can amount to family dramas when individuals want to change their identity. In most cases, this happens through marriage. Ms. Marusa Popa, of lipovan origin, recalls the problems she and her sisters had when married. Being the nieces of the lipovan priests, for them marrying outside the community was out of the question. Measures of prevention included beating, punishing and grounding the girl to force her to marry a lipovan. She was herself the third sister to marry a Romanian, a final and unforgivable sin in the eyes of her parents, who eventually threw her out of the house. However, she recalls, in a very humorous manner, the process: *"The Romanian orthodox priest baptized me with one drop of kitchen oil, for he had forgotten the holy oil at home. And then he said: There you go, you're a Romanian. And thus, with three crosses and a drop of kitchen oil I became a Romanian"*. Beyond her irony, however, there are particular tensions and dramas, as people can feel pressured by the lipovan priest, who is very strict and refuses to bury them or pay religious services if the believers do not attend regularly the church or loosen/lose faith.

In short, after the dissolution of CED and the rather artificial multicultural way of life it produced, Sulina witnessed a rearrangement of social values and connections. While ethnic stereotyping still persists, although not bluntly, the label can be occasionally changed or loosen up if the individual performs better socially: a lipovan with a good job and/or reputation can be respected and accepted, but he will never be "from a good family" like a Greek. Otherwise, ethnic stereotyping can always be a good outlet when people are upset: "Go back to your Brejnev!" can be yelled at a Lipovan, alluding to their Russian origin. In some cases, older informants refer to social stratification before the war, with the Greeks being the superior "class". One informant coming from a mixed family (Romanian father, Greek mother) recalls that most Greeks used to despise Romanians for being "polenta eaters full of lice". When her father was courting the mother, the Greek grandmother used to announce in absolute contempt: "The peasant is here".

Another interesting aspect is that most people in Sulina had nicknames, referring either to their ethnic origin, or their occupation: one informant, former fisherman, had the nickname of *Zaiț* ("rabbit" in Russian, as he used to be a very good dancer of cazachok), another one was called *Ciortika* (meaning "little devil" in Russian, as he was of a small height and full of energy). Also, people were used to scorn each other, especially in the case of close groups. One informant describes how this mechanism of mutual mockery functioned in the case of three neighboring villages: *"There was a saying, that if you want to eat well, you go to Letea [Ukrainian village], if you want to drink well, you go to C. A. Rosetti [Moldavian village], and if you want to have sex, you go to Sfistofca [Lipovan village, where girls were famous for their beauty]"* (Teampău 2011: 84–85). Another informant has a different version about other villages: *"People in Sf. Gheorghe are called "chishmani" (meaning fish bowels), those in Caraorman, "cabaci" (meaning pumpkins, because they had gardens and were selling pumpkins), those in Letea "baclajani" (from the potatoes they were selling in the market), and those in C. A. Rosetti were called "cojani", meaning shepherds. These were kind of offensive and they would use it against each other in a fight"* (Teampău 2013: 69–70). We suggest that these mockeries are relevant for the quiescent tensions that exist between different groups, especially where they compete for resources, but at the same time can function as a sort of depressurization, letting off steam instead of resorting to explicit violence.

We have often observed in Sulina confusion on cultural identity. In positive terms, the hybridism of the margin produced blurred boundaries in most everyday situations. The groups that were clearly identifiable under the CED have either gone or merged in complex patterns, with 'Romanian' emerging as the dominating identity. In prewar Sulina, interactions between those groups could be studied, the patterns of interactions could be studied as performances of multiculturalism, but presently, both discourses from above (tourism, policy, etc.) and the truly hybrid/confused character of ethnic identity make the palimpsest of multiculturalism extremely hard to read.

Pressures to be Romanian in the first place increased with communism, and only slightly diminished after communism. The value of being Lipovan or speaking Russian changed. The appreciation of Armenian links could change quickly. The story of Sulina as a cosmopolitan place serves as a positive orientation for the future, but also as a way to rethink the past without much pressure of visible traces of the past. The story can hold more sway because of the fractured identities, or in other cases less prestigious identities of the people actually living in the town. It becomes more attractive since the alternatives are not great and since there is a great plasticity. In the presence of discourses of nature conservation, it also acquires a new value as a counter-weight, as an alternative image, not in tune with the stories of untouched nature promoted by the green actors.

The cosmopolitan version most prevalent, is clearly structured by the fantasies of the present, inspired by what is desirable and what is absent. The CED past is presented as a period of plenty, of no interest in nature, of unrestrained development, of centrality, rich information, personal development and of peaceful coexistence between various groups. Few talk about the groups mixing, rather about discrete elements fully enjoying distinct identities. The money came from 'Europe' and 'Europe' is expected to bring it back. The European interest in nature conservation in the area is thus not well understood, and experienced as disappointing.

6.2 Gatekeepers and Promoters of Memory

Social memory is not an object but a series of processes; if they stop, memory unravels. Memory is continuously transformed in these processes. If places lose diversity, importance and embedding in global networks, cosmopolitanism relies more on memory, but also when centrality was never lost, social memory continuously reconstructs the local versions of cosmopolitanism. It reconstructs what is typical for the community, why it is cosmopolitan, what is good about it, and what is cosmopolitanism as such-even if there is no direct reflection on the concept.

What can be presented as cosmopolitanism changes over time, and the answers to the questions of how and why also differ. Places with a cosmopolitan history tend to cherish this, yet mold the stories according to internal and external demands. Forcing Armenians to settle in a Persian town is not accepted anymore,

6.2 Gatekeepers and Promoters of Memory

and the resulting form of cosmopolitanism will not be loudly announced right now. But the story can be changed, and their presence can be part of a story of peaceful coexistence in ancient Persia. Social memory never exists completely outside the state, that is, without a relation to narratives, identities and connections promoted by the state. For CED this is obvious, but one can make a more general claim here. The state can be local, as with Venice, and it can be an empire, as with Trieste. What is remembered is more thoroughly transformed in modern nation states, with their pressures of homogeneity, their school systems, religious policies etc. (Magris 1988; Simonsen 2008). Yet in other political entities, there are still necessary links between what and how things are remembered, and what the political system thinks and wants, how it sees itself, its environment, its current and ideal constituents. If communities are structured in a political sense, if we can speak of governance, as the taking of collectively binding decisions, then these decisions tough on identities in various ways, on their histories and the way they fit the political image of self. Similarly, governance affects networks which enable certain forms of cosmopolitanism, and bring certain selectivities of memory.

Individual agency remains important. We have to mention the functions of gatekeepers and promoters of memory, in general and in the case of Sulina. The state, or influential players in governance, can function as gatekeepers or promoters (negative and positive selectivities), yet people can be influential on memory matters without such affiliation (Van Assche and Teampău 2009). The influence can be associated with a religious role, a spiritual role, but also more simply with the value placed on a particular version of history by other actors, and the rarity of that version.

Because in Sulina the transformation was so extreme, and silence was so oppressive under communism, very few people were able after communism to give substance to generic narratives or even fragmentary narratives about a glorious cosmopolitan past under the CED. So many things had changed, so few people could be linked to the era, and if so, they identified in different ways, or, if not, their ancestors had not been in a position to experience much of the cosmopolitan character of old Sulina (Teampău and Van Assche 2009b). The new value of the old Sulina story made the search intensive, but reliant on recirculating tropes and commonplaces, on some old architecture which remained silent for most, besides a generic reference to wealth, taste, to faraway places. Very strong promotion of memory is tough since there are so few direct links, and the story is repeated but not entirely convincing for all. It leaves space however for a strong role for a gatekeeper of memory (Van Assche et al. 2009).

Memory can be accompanied by archive as the source of new memories, but for Sulina, the transformation that made actual recall hard also scattered and destroyed the archives. A large part of the CED archives apparently burned during WWII, and the rest is fragmented and resting in various European archives, from Paris to Vienna. Nevertheless, locally, there are a few archival efforts, going back to different points in time, and using different means, sometimes tied to ethnic or cultural identities, sometimes tied to 'Sulina' as the overarching story. A Lipovan (Russian speaking Old Believer) historical society and a collector and maker of

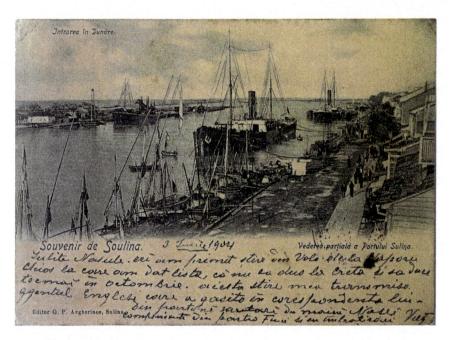

Fig. 6.2 Vintage postcard of the harbor of Sulina (dated by sender 9 June 1904), hand-written in Romanian. The sender writes to his godfather about business in crete and news received "through the correspondence of the English agent". [Public domain]

photographs try to document the changing character of Sulina. The municipal archive does not go back very far and contains scarce references to the cosmopolitan heydays (Fig. 6.2).

For a more persuasive story about old Sulina, the town relied for many years on a Greek gentleman, mr Zachis, unfortunately recently deceased (Teampău 2010). He represented the memory of the CED times for many players, locally and elsewhere. His role in the community was special. He was consulted by locals and visitors alike, was present at occasions celebrating Sulina's history, culture, diversity, and gave credibility to an otherwise tenuous connection with a desired past. There are various aspects to the function of 'gatekeeper of memory', and the implications for narrative dynamics in the community and the local construction of cosmopolitanism are diverse. His story was not simply 'believed', as in taken for granted and replacing alternatives. Rather, there was an acknowledgment of the value of the connection and the stories. In Peircean terms, mr Zachis was a scarce source of indexicality, of contiguity: this person here is from here and embodies this history of here. Such link of connections made the past more real, and not too much emphasis was placed on the relations between his cosmopolitan story and other stories (Van Assche 2004). Yet, at the same time, we cannot say that his story was entirely instrumentalized for political or economic reasons. People also want to identify with the Sulina emerging from his stories, stories made real by his presence and telling of them. Yet the link is still tenuous, and the alternative sources of identification are still strong, local, and hard to ignore. One cannot simply erase a Lipovan identity in a small community, or give such identity a privileged place in a CED cosmopolitan narrative. Stories will be told and retold, emphasizing the cosmopolitan character, but there is bound to remain some distance, an occasional character to the identification. The stories helped to strengthen the resolve to restore buildings, which in turn reinforces the cosmopolitan narrative, increases its believability.

Some stories are meant to explicitly show how important Sulina was, at the same time adding some local colour: for instance, the recurrent narrative which attributes to the Queen of Netherlands the building of the Water Tower. The story goes that she visited Sulina at the beginning of the XXth century (ca 1910) and asked for a glass of water, which she received straight from the Danube [the local colour: some people still drink water straight form the Danube, and also, they say that the best traditional fish soup has to be made with the same water]. The queen was horrified, and she immediately donated the money to build a water plant which is still currently in use and filters the running water for the entire city (cf. Zachis narrative, Teampău 2009: 32).

In general, Zachis remembered a wealth of (often technical) details about life during the CED period (shipbuilding, commerce), while glossing over some of the less appealing aspects. He remembered stories about other Greeks in Sulina, and fragments of stories about his Greek relatives abroad, but even for him, the closed narrative worlds of Romanian communism and of his marginal, eccentric town, made it really hard to make sense of the Greek presence and experience in Sulina. Everything is subsumed under the master-narrative, and storylines on the various ethnic groups are not developed, even if one identifies proudly with one of them (see also Teampău and Van Assche 2009a: 62).

The CED period reappears over and over again in the stories of the local people. The era is glorified in many ways: population numbers are consistently exaggerated (people mention 40,000, 50,000, 60,000, when in reality it was around 10,000; Rosetti et al. 2006[1931]; Mihailescu and Vulpe 1940). The wealth is exaggerated: unskilled laborers are imagined in the restaurants daily: 'every morning, they had a steak at the restaurant, before they got to work'. The multicultural and harmonious character is stressed many times, disregarding the sharp social distinctions: 'there were no problems, no conflict, everyone respected each other; they all lived in harmony'. [...]Very often, poignant descriptions of poverty and conflict fill the historical narratives, and the barely experienced CED period offers an almost blank page that can be filled by the desire for the inverse, for prosperity and harmony (Van Assche et al. 2009: 226).

On one hand, Zachis's narrative has a realist framing, in which he acknowledges the crucial importance of CED, but then he goes on to tell fabulous stories about the wealth and good life of Sulina without linking them to the temporality of the CED project. *"What can I say? If they didn't decide back then to establish the European Commission of Danube, Sulina wouldn't have been what it is today. [...] We had 42 food stores, and also many-many tailor's shops, hairdresser's, woodwork, restaurants etc. We had absolutely everything, we didn't lack anything"* [...] *We had three printing houses, which were printing in 6–7 languages, starting with English, Greek, and French and so on, because, as Jean Bart said, Sulina used to be a cosmopolitan city. We had nine consulates, British, French, Greek, Turkish, and Italian. If you want I can tell you the names of each of their representatives. There were so many ships coming in, under different colours, and all of their problems had to be solved through consulates. We also had a bank, where one could exchange currency. If so many ships came, they had perhaps 10–15 different citizenships, each with its own currency!"* (Teampău 2009: 33, 38).

He describes a city which was certainly caught in a network of good connections to the outside world: *"We had very good connections through the ships that were travelling all over the world and were bringing back goods for the local stores: "Ardealul", "Peles", "Carpati", "Alba Iulia", "Cavarna", "Balcic", "Sulina" etc. People who wanted to travel to Italy, Greece, Turkey, they left with a simple document, that was actually a piece of paper written by hand, with an instant picture, saying where and for how long they go. All they needed was a stamp, and they could go. That was the personal passport"* (Teampău 2009: 49). Also: *"There were passengers' ships and commercial ships, and they would bring all possible merchandise from all over the world, such as nutmeg, vanilla, pepper, dates, lemons, oranges, cinnamon, figs, bay. We had special spices shops, when you entered, the smell was overwhelming"* (Teampău 2009: 55, 2010).

Of course, the main tone of the story-telling is enjoyable and optimistic, as the narrator speaks about his youth, and there are stories about serenades and mouthwatering cookies and nice places, but all of them reinforce the idea of multiculturalism and prosperity: *"When we were young, we used to sing serenades for beautiful girls, and there were many beautiful girls in Sulina: especially Turkish, but also Italian, Greek. The songs were also so nice. We sang in Greek, in Russian, in Italian, equally. Honestly, if you didn't speak these languages here, you could hardly get by. We sang in several languages to all the girls, because they all knew them"* (Teampău 2009: 43–44). *"Oh, the pastry shops! I've never had anything like that ever since. I remember some places: Apesos, Vlahos, Vasiliadis, Cochinos. Coffeshops: Sefki, Vitoratos, Muriotis, Alipranti, Delighiorghi, Baziotis Iani, Makris, Barbatis, Psaludis, Jalba, Vidovici Vido, Grigorean, Lufidis Gherasim, Trigonis Iani, Sacalov, Psaludis Panaiota. What can I say: this was a city that had everything!"* (Teampău 2009: 64). Even nature and the surroundings showed the impact of Sulina's opening and networks: *"There was the CED park, with beautiful flowers. The employees would bring back from their homelands all kinds of seeds, and had flowers here from England, Denmark. They had their own gardeners, and their own tennis court. Also, there was a skating instructor specially for the CED employees, Iani Barbatis"* (Teampău 2009: 79, 2010).

In the end, Zachis returns to his attempt at providing a realistic account of Sulina during CED, but without a clear understanding of what CED was outside Sulina: *"I said it before and I will say it again a thousand times: If it weren't for CED, Sulina wouldn't be what it was. It was a huge enterprise. It was the only one who had the courage to assume responsibility for making the Danube navigable.*

They met there in Paris and said: "Well, this is who we are, this is what we can do and we'll do it!" and they did it. And today we have a navigable Danube and a straight Danube. [...] Since its establishment up until 1939 when it left, CED was for this city like a family. It gave Sulina the shape of a city" (Teampău 2009: 98, 101). *"Jean Bart has written that Sulina was a cosmopolitan city. True! In fact, it was only because of CED. They had special demands, and our village was not up to them so they had to satisfy them themselves, and they started building"* (Teampău 2009: 98, 107). After CED left (1939), the networks dissolved also, almost instantly, and the communist regime forbad any mention of the presence of "imperialist powers": *"The foreigners from CED, they all left. My father received for a while postcards from Mr. Magnus and Mr. Rosiny, both engineers at CED, very good people, but only until the war. Afterwards, with the communists, nothing! They were censoring everything, all mail"* (Teampău 2009: 98, 118).

In the end, Zachis concludes the narrative with a pragmatist note, which reasserts the impossibility of return or of replicating the good times of Sulina. The narrative remains enclosed in a mythical framework, which reinforces its power as absolute reference: *"I do not think that what used to be in Sulina will ever come back: the value of money, the good work provided by CED, the harbor, the fishing, and a good and cheap life. There are so many other things that could be said, but for some, these are just stories, not lives lived in this city. There was a time when in Sulina you could walk around in the fancy carriage pulled by horses with colorful bells, owned by Politis, Manolachi, Antimaritis or Manolatos, or with the taxi driven by Samsonica or Hagiopol, or the truck of Hursut brothers. You could listen to the fanfare in the park or in front of the restaurant of Parparia Camberi, or go to the famous parties offered in the building of the Greek Cinema by the Romanian Naval League. These all remain just memories about what Sulina used to be. Never to return"* (Teampău 2009: 98, 156–157).

A detailed understanding of social memory sheds a different light on the functions of the versions of local cosmopolitanism, within Sulina and in confrontations with actors at larger scales. In Sulina, what can be remembered and what is remembered thoroughly shape the local cosmopolitanism, because it is so thoroughly absent in the daily life of people. Locals are proud to say that a century ago, locals knew about the news in Paris, but the locals now have little connection with the old ones, and the mechanisms and networks that brought Paris to Sulina have changed in ways eluding the same storytelling locals.

When groups and networks dissolve, no longer communicate and exchange information in daily life and through collective rituals, they slowly lose the capacity to revive and actualize their social identity and memory. Information and meaning used in everyday culture, politics, trade and economic life disappears from social networks; networks break down and/or the position of places in the networks shifts. In such a process of marginalization, resources, people and information are lost. People redefine themselves; groups restructure their narratives; the local economy, politics, even religion redefines itself, *and there is no way of 'getting it back'*, since there is nothing to retrieve or revisit. The starting point in the past, the point in time before marginalization started, is a vantage point lost forever, and the picture of reality and past realities that could once be captured has faded away. Identities, narratives and other frames once producing knowledge are gone or changed (Esposito 2002; Irwin-Zarecka 1994; cf. Van Assche et al. 2009: 218).

Some of the more recent players on the scene are also promoters of versions of memory, sometimes the cosmopolitan past, sometimes the existence on the edge of the world, or its place in the middle of a sublime 'natural' area, the marshlands of the Danube delta. We mentioned before that local cosmopolitanism in Sulina is also a response to stories of marginality and stories of an unspoiled natural character, which for many locals reinforces the marginality story. Only tourism entrepreneurs and promoters (e.g. some people in local government) seem to succeed in combining stories of nature with stories of a cosmopolitan past. The reason seems to be that for tourism, both can be of value, and secondly, that cosmopolitanism is firmly placed in the past, without much repercussion for the present, without inspiring new hopes for the future. Tourism and the commodification of memory alter the discursive dynamics in the community.

Nationalism and EU enlargement also play out, and influence the memory selections taking place, and the forms and functions of local cosmopolitanism. As said, the area was an unstable margin for Romania for a long time, an external and later internal margin. People did not identify as Romanian, histories were deep, identities old, and more prestigious in some ways than what the young Romanian state could offer. Romanization was intense until the end of the communist period, with people moved in, pushed out, and pushed to change. Nationalism never disappeared during communism, and revived with the long hoped for arrival of the European Union in 2007 (Teampău and Van Assche 2007a, b; Van Assche et al. 2011a, b).

We can see the "European destiny" of Sulina underlined in a more or less coherent narrative of a local sailor, who is particularly passionate about the history of the city. He emphasizes the idea that not only was Sulina a blend of ethnicities, languages and religious confessions, but also, beyond metaphors, it was an amalgam of soils brought from all over the world, but especially Europe. In his view, Europe literally came down here: *When ships came from they were loaded with gravel, sand or other materials from their homelands for ballast, and when they crossed over the sand bar at the channel entrance, they unloaded the gravel and put it in the city where the swamps were drained. So we have here a conglomerate of soils brought here from all over Europe; maybe we even have soils from Africa, who knows? So just as we had here people of all possible nations, so is the land on which we sit gathered from all over Europe, or the world. Over the swamp that was here 300–400 years ago, we have now land from all over Europe. In my opinion, Sulina was the grandmother of European Union. Sulina wasn't always the little town it is today, but a harbour with important ties and connections with other harbours and the entire Europe. The best European commercial businesses came down here* (Teampău 2013: 59). Surely, it works beautifully as a metaphor for the blend of ethnicities and cultures that Sulina certainly was at a time and for a while, but it does not critically understand and assess the whole context for this European project, its meaning, and most importantly, its provisional nature (Fig. 6.3).

SULINA • SOSIREA VAPORULUI DE PASAGERI

Fig. 6.3 Vintage interwar postcard of Sulina, printed in Romanian "The arrival of the passengers ship". Times have changed, but the arrival of the passenger ship is still a daily event for the locals, especially in the summer season. [Public domain]

One can say that at this moment, the future of the town is seen, once again, in connection to the European project. The almost mythical prosperity of the Danube Commission period is being projected into the near future, when Sulina will be a "European" city, in a kind of cyclical fate (Teampău and Van Assche 2007a, b: 273).

Also, Romanian media constantly portray Sulina as a dead place, but a place with a glorious past, stating explicitly that "European Union was born in Sulina, 150 years ago, since through here Europe has entered Romania. In Sulina, it is proven with tombstones that we have been in Europe since a long time". Retrospectively, Sulina of those happy times "when Europe was floating on Danube", is "remembered" as a place of abundance, an El Dorado, "a city where a simple worker was earning every day enough money to feed 30 people at the restaurant. O locality integrated in Europe, with no unemployment" (*Adevărul*, 23. 08. 2005). All of these events are being projected by newspapers in a mythical time, with undertones that make things seem at least unreal: "As soon as the first Europeans landed in the middle of reed [...] and the European money started to flow in the city faster than the waters of Danube into the sea, the life of the place took off as nowhere else in the country. A simple porter in the harbor would earn 500 lei per day. In the morning, before going to work, he would eat a steak at the restaurant and drink a bottle of red wine for only 15 lei". Moreover, there were theaters, cafes, and, of course, brothels (*Jurnalul național*, 26. 06. 2006).

It is easy to observe that most references of a good living revolve around urban entertainment: eating at restaurants and participating in an urban public life. Also, speaking about the "life of the place" is no hazard; it is meant to emphasize again, by way of comparison, the death of this city in our days (cf. Teampău and Van Assche 2007a, b: 273).

In fact, EU accession came with pressures, with new rules, with a feeling of being treated as second rate citizens, with a hardening of the border, now an EU border, and a militarization through the presence of a revamped border police in the formerly more unobserved margin. For Sulina specifically, Europe thus came as a paradox, offering new closures and openings to the larger world. The new EU was not the CED, and locals had difficulties in distinguishing the two. Nostalgia for a barely known CED was projected on a barely known EU, and the failure to bring immediate riches brought a disappointment with the EU which translated into a not very strong motivation to reinvent governance and move forwards in new ways. Europe did not recognize its lost child Sulina, and the Sulinese. Europe had forgotten the CED too, as well as Sulina. Rather than being perceived as a prodigal son, Sulina was a small liability, on a tricky border, in a supposedly natural area.

6.3 A History of Marginality

If we take the angle of networks, of economic, political and cultural networks, then the position of Sulina can be described as initially marginal, central under CED, and marginal again recently.

Sulina under the Ottomans was not important, as we know. We called the local architecture Ottoman, but this implies little reference to the architectural innovations at the center. Ottoman learning ignored the place, as did the main networks of trade. In the later middle ages, the 14th and early 15th centuries, Genovese traders were active in the Danube Delta, and a short term revival of Silk Road connections could be observed. But once the Ottomans took over in the 1450s, the Delta became a backwater again (Ascherson 2007). Also militarily, the border was not important since the other side of the river was Crimean Tatar territory, a vassal state and a buffer state against Russia and the Polish-Lithuanian commonwealth. Immigration into the Delta was, as we mentioned, mostly a flight to the margins, to uncontrolled and unobserved margins. When Peter the Great persecuted Old Believers in the early 18th centuries, but also later, those conservative Orthodox Christians fled to the margins of the Russian empire, where they could observe their religion (Stricker 1990; Subtelny 2009; King 2004). They arrived in Siberia, Alaska, but also the Danube Delta. Cossacks, from the Don area among others, had a deeply ambiguous relation with the empire, sometimes working for them, sometimes hiding, sometimes escaping. They too ended up in the Delta.

The Tatars were ethnically mixed already, and in the marshlands on the margin, several Russian and Ukrainian speaking groups arrived which can now be hardly distinguished. There were several versions of Old Believers, several Cossack groups, and also fishermen and farmers who spoke one of these languages, one of their dialectics, without falling easily into Cossack or Old Believer categories. In some periods, the Ottomans granted new Russian arrivals privileges as long as they defended the border. We already mentioned that the 18th century saw Russian colonization starting the other side of the river, even before Crimea was conquered (King 2004). The border slowly stabilized and turned less permeable, but movement of fishing groups was still frequent until the Russian revolution. The people living there were less oppressed in some ways, less enfranchised in others. Only with communist (competing) regimes two sides of the border, a concerted effort at linking up the margin with the center, and at developing these margins was undertaken (Van Assche and Teampău 2010).

Work conducted at the Danube Delta National Institute for Research and Development indicates that in the last century alone, the Old Believers moved from five ethnic groups to two and now one (personal communications at DDNI, Sulina; unpublished manuscripts kept at DDNI). Some vanished distinctions were prominent in the past, as is common among Christian denominations elsewhere. The marginal position, and the tumultuous histories, made ethnic categories function differently. Social memories were rewritten fast, in this landscape under pressure, under political pressure and under physical pressure of a river and a sea easily erasing all landmarks and transforming all useful spots. What could be done in the place changed, while boundaries would move, Russian armies could raze villages, floods, new people would come in, others would move to the more fertile farmland south and west of the marshes. Also there, Old Believer (locally called Lipovan) villages existed, but others would see that move as another opportunity to redefine themselves. The margin was therefore also functional, in the sense of a refuge that was at the same time a portal and a pressure cooker. Villages did not exist for long, and categories and identities did not exist for long. Opportunities were scarce.

When the Romanian communists came to the scene, the Delta was still a suspicious place, close to the USSR and to the part of old Romania, Moldova, that was taken away by the USSR (Boia 2001; Verdery 1991). It was still a place of suspicious cultural diversity and of lacking state control. Under Ceauşescu, as we know, Romanians from other regions were moved in, industrialization was started, communist style apartment blocks partially replaced the CED architecture, and, especially since the 1970s, more comprehensive plans towards development of the Delta were drawn up. Canals were built, salty marshes reclaimed and turned into pastures, marshlands turned into river polders (Van Assche et al. 2008). The communists built fish farms, partly using the natural landscape, partly relying on artificial ponds. Reed production was scaled up and turned into an industrial enterprise. Many of these attempts were not very successful, but up to the fall of communism, the attempts never stopped and the failures were not admitted.

Sulina was an island, a broad river levy that was artificially enlarged and connected with the dry dune areas. In the 1970s, the isolated position was softened by a land reclamation project to the south. Original spatial boundaries have been softened, connections slightly improved, but Sulina remains an inaccessible place. The Sulina canal, result of CED projects, is hardly in use anymore, and as a seaport, Constanta has taken over completely. Since the collapse of the CED and certainly since WW II, the Greek, Jewish, Armenian trading communities have disappeared, and with them, their networks, their embeddings in a larger world. Communism tried to keep people here, by founding new industries, for mostly Lipovan workers, but these enterprises did not last. There was a Fish Canning Factory, built in the '70s, that attracted many workers, mostly from the villages but also from Moldova, and the Naval Shipyard that employed more than 500 men. Nowadays, the population shrinks fast, unemployment is over 50 %, and all kinds of semi-legal operations are rampant. Half-jokingly, administrators in Tulcea say that nobody in Sulina pays taxes, and if you do, you're the laughing stock of the neighborhood. A newly invigorated border police (EU influence), also responsible for Sulina, seems to have a positive impact now on certain aspects of law enforcement (cf. Van Assche et al. 2008: 127–128).

People do have a sort of nostalgia for the communist period, where some of them had a good life. One informant speaks about "a second romantic period of Sulina, after CED, in the '70s–'80s", when life had a new start: the communist authorities were investing in Sulina, they were building new working places, everyone was employed etc. The Fish Factory was built in 1970 and started producing the first cans in 1973, with local fish and local recipes. One informant who worked there since its inception says: "*It hurts my heart to see how it was destroyed. That factory was built to last 300 years, and it only lasted 30. The building is still there, but it stands like a ghost, as a sing of futility*" (Teampău 2013: 78). During communism, the Factory was an important asset: not only that over 500 people, mostly women, were working there, in three shifts, but also everyone was benefiting, one way or another, from it: "*Everyone was eating there, or from there. You know, a little bit of oil, of something, and those who worked shared it with the neighbours, so nobody was starving, everyone had something. I would not call it stealing, it's not stealing; we only took little bottles of oil and give a drop to others, also*" (Teampău 2013: 88). Some people tried to live as in a bubble, just using the local resources and having a good life. "*We did not care that it was communism, that there was Ceaușescu, and what he did. Why should we have cared, here, in Sulina. We did not know and we did not talk about Ceaușescu, we only cared about our job. I worked at this hotel and I was responsible for the people who came there, not Ceaușescu. I'm telling you, it was a good life, and a good life for all*" (Teampău 2013: 96). The presumed isolation is also relapsed, as Sulina seemed to be a knot: "We were not isolated, as one might think. Sulina is the first harbour of Danube, you have a connection with other people, with all the countries in the world, America, Australia, you name it. All those ships were coming here" (Teampău 2013: 104).

Sulina was the exception in the Danube Delta because of its CED period. That period was only possible because of a particular geopolitical situation already sketched, because of diasporic minorities with Eastern networks already mentioned (Jews, Armenians, Greeks), and because of a western interest going beyond

6.3 A History of Marginality

conflict prevention (England wanted wheat). The cemetery at Sulina testifies to that past, with English, Greek, Armenian, Tatar, Ukrainian, Russian, French and other graves close to each other. The CED brought expertise networks (engineering), trade connections, political connections, and a development strategy as a new form of coordination of policies and practices eying a different future. Learning was encouraged, schools sponsored. When it ended, slowly, after a period of marginalization of the CED itself, what was left were memories, some architecture, but also some people who would otherwise not be there. People who took root or could not escape. There were still some Greeks, a few Armenians, very few Jews after World War II, despite the chaos of the war years, deportations, and Romanization campaigns.

New expertise came in, through schools in Tulcea, and access for some to universities in Bucharest and elsewhere, as well as investigations into the Delta sponsored by the regime. There were newspapers, radio, later TV, but in a more closed society, in which it occupied a marginal place. Despite modernization campaigns, many people in the Delta lived in huts similar to those improvised by their ancestors arriving there a few centuries earlier. Fish moved quickly to Bucharest, but that was probably the tightest connection one can find (Van Assche et al. 2011a, b). What was going on in the Delta, remained mysterious for much of the communist era. The success of development plans was not announced widely, the prison camps were not supposed to exist, the surviving poverty and other social problems were not supposed to be there. A commonplace was that vodka is the real currency in the Delta, another one that memories don't exist, that people don't remember what happened there three days ago. The perception of marginality coexisted with a self-perception of marginality, a lack of identification with the regime-proudly proclaiming to be descendants of pirates, e.g. (Van Assche et al. 2008, 2009). With international connections cut off, and the actual port moved south of the Delta, Sulina and the Delta became dependent on the mainland, with Tulcea being the regional capital, about 100 km west, about a day in small boat. Tulcea was not interested in Sulina, and center and periphery turned around. The better schools, trade connections, political connections were now (and still are) in Tulcea. Under communism already, Sulina and the surrounding marshland villages were emptying out, first into Tulcea, and people later moving on to other regions and into diaspora. Even now, most young people want to move out, many tried, and few see a prosperous future for themselves in Sulina.

The actual functioning of networks, the disembedding of Sulina from networks, its throwback on very local networks (even the region is foreign territory), has economic, cultural and political implications. Stories about European products from the CED era are part of the imaginary of lost cosmopolitanism, and stories about the lousy communist products demonstrate the lack of identification with that regime. Greeks maintained connections with Greece and the Mediterranean up to the War, bringing in products, cultural innovations, but also this source was cut off. The rich Jewish world spanning the Mediterranean, Black Sea and Central Europe lost its connectivity in a sadly obvious sense when it lost its people. Armenia was redefined more and more as the small Soviet Republic, forcibly forgetting that the ancient homeland was elsewhere and bigger. Armenian networks in the USSR thrived, but not in Romania. Both new ideas and new things, as well as people, moved more slowly and sparsely (Smith 1998).

It has implications, again, for narrative dynamics, for the nostalgic patina of local cosmopolitanism, for the potential of mythologizing cosmopolitanism, and for the difficulty in reviving internal diversity and wider embedding. We spoke already of the tenuous connection with the CED history, and the lacking resistance against radical reinvention of cosmopolitan narratives. When we add the networked marginality, we can understand that finding other sources for local history is hard, and that comparing with other places, other cosmopolitan places, is hard. That makes it hard to understand how internal diversity and larger networks were important to produce a form of local cosmopolitanism where narrative and network can somehow be matched, in a way that increases stability and coordination (Jacobs and Van Assche 2014). It makes it tougher to understand the peculiar conditions, locally, regionally and internationally, which led to the CED success, and thus to the difficulties in recreating these conditions.

The history of marginality, and the vanishing of the networks and groups associated with centrality, has its impact on the stories told about past, present and future, on the narrative resources available and the forces shaping the narrative (Van Assche et al. 2008; Teampău and Van Assche 2009b). Marginality creates desire, and it creates desires that are often not very well grounded in an understanding of success, e.g. in the form of a cosmopolitan past and future. We know now that in Sulina, the marginalization of Sulina and its narrative presence have to be related to the age old marginality of the surrounding marshes. The delta has been a marginal place for centuries, a place literally on the margin, the margin of land and sea, of swamp and sea, of empires and the power of their political centers. People unfriendly to these political centers found refuge in the swamps. The marshes and their islands offered opportunities to hide, to live a quiet life, to maintain an ethnic identity problematic elsewhere, and it was an environment in which ethnic categories blurred in new and unexpected ways (Van Assche et al. 2011a, b). Most current residents of Sulina trace their ancestry in the surrounding marshes, and beyond that in places beyond the horizon or at least beyond the border. Histories of marginality mix sometimes easily sometimes uneasily with cosmopolitan narratives; marginal pasts give a new lure to the CED stories, they can also inspire a proud story of a life of piracy in the shadow of the law, and these histories can inspire a reinterpretation, or a new version, of the cosmopolitan narrative, in which the aspect of 'free port' becomes essential, in a spirit of freebooting and adventurism.

Another aspect of marginality needs to be mentioned here: the limited control from the centre. Recently, with increasing Romanian education, the conceptual boundaries of Romanian culture are more dominant, but with the older generations, the influence of education is lower, and concomitantly, the influence of Romanian categorizations and discourses. Before Romania felt the need for strict border control and had the means to do so, the border, as spatial boundary was often not very relevant for the local communities. More slowly, the force of law,

6.3 A History of Marginality

including fighting tax evasion, was extended to the boundary zone, the swamps. Even now, tax evasion and other cracks in the law are major concerns for all the regional administrations, and it is often admitted that the problems have not been solved at all. Finding out real income is hard, even population statistics are hard to come by. From the perspective of the administrations, a history of marginality, a tradition of soft or absent law, a tradition of freedom, explains the present difficulties with law enforcement. All of this being reinforced by the nature of the landscape, the vast marshes, and by the physical distance from effective power centers (see also Van Assche et al. 2008: 126, 127).

Marginality is one major element in the identity narrative of Lipoveni. On one hand, they ended up in the swamp looking for place to hide, on the other hand, many of their villages in the Delta, places they lived in before coming to Sulina, had short histories, an ephemeral existence, and the variety of groups that filtered into the Delta area all had different histories and reasons to move. Result is a confused history, and a social memory that is extremely simplified ('we came when Peter cut the beards') and, for many of them, not entirely convincing—people do express their doubts after relating the story, or tell it with hesitation (cf. Van Assche and Teampău 2009: 15). Not even the head of the Lipovan Organization in Sulina, mr. Halchin, does not have a more detailed account of how they came here, but his narrative is one of persecutions and flight: *"Lipoveni have been through a lot until today. When they left Russia the Czar was persecuting them, they kept running, then the Turks persecuted them, they kept running, and so they ended up in the swamp and stayed there. There's a paradox: we say we are Russian, but the old ones have been running away from Russian all their lives. We are, so to speak, the first dissidents. It's one thing when you have a population that was sedentary for centuries and another when you have to keep running. That is why they have always been so poor: they never had time to become wealthy. If one generation lived in a place, the second or the third generation had to move. And just like the gypsies, they put everything on boats, including the deconstructed church, and flew. They needed the church, because everything they had was in the church: the celebrations, Christmas, everything"* (Teampău 2011: 90–91).

6.4 New Borders and Boundaries

The narratives of identification that cannot be disassociated from local cosmopolitanism are in turn shaped by concepts of boundaries. We distinguish between social, spatial and conceptual boundaries, and reflect on their interactions, and the consequences for narratives and practices of cosmopolitanism (Jacobs and Van Assche 2014; Van Assche et al. 2008). For us, all boundaries are conceptual, since nothing is a boundary without a boundary concept. Natural boundaries are only boundaries when they are perceived to function as such, when there is a systematic reference to that perception. Mountains and rivers are natural boundaries, but also unities and connectors, for people and for natural life. They are obstacles without biologists and geographers designating them as obstacles, indeed, but for us, they can only be obstacles when there is a concept to understand them as obstacles (and not as challenge, opportunity, or as blank resistance). Whereas in the case of obstacles, boundaries as obstacles, one could still make the case that resistance is the experience of boundary, and that this precedes signification, we can say less controversially that a broader boundary concept, as something delineating something else, needs an understanding of that something else. One could say that resistance and obstacle and imply contiguity, still requiring a sign but an indexical sign directly linked to what it signified, boundary properly understood relies less on indexicality and more on symbolization (Van Assche 2004).

Boundaries can start symbolization and they can be the result of relations discovered and symbolized first. A boundary defines what is inside, and it can be defined first by a set of relations or shared features observed in a spatial or conceptual landscape. Something physical can inspire the spatial boundary, but whether that is natural, or the result of previous human activities, or a greater sensitivity to a line or obstacle because of a history of symbolization, can never be entirely disentangled. This is not a problem, neither in practice nor for theory. Something functions as a boundary, and has boundary effects on two sides of itself (Luhmann 1995). What interests us more here is that spatial, conceptual and social boundaries transform and imply each other.

Spatial boundaries, projected by a group, can define a group, while the group will over time change these spatial boundaries in conceptual and spatial sense, by conquering territory and redefining and reinterpreting the boundary. Boundaries which were economic and political can become more cultural, while cultural boundaries can fade away, leaving a line only as an administrative demarcation, even without much political effect beyond the demarcation and its effects on political calculus and aggregation. Groups change when they move around, encounter other places, other people, and when they are locked up in a ghetto. They change when they engage in learning and trade, when they enter different conceptual territory (Van Assche et al. 2013; Van Assche and Hornidge 2014). A new religion can bring a new philosophy which holds the seeds for concepts which enable new form of trade later, trade facilitated by moving political boundaries and by a new willingness to redefine the group, to marry others outside the group, to learn from them (Verdery 1991). Social boundaries in more intricate, convoluted, folded forms, as identities allowing for contextual use, for ambiguity, for reinvention and bricolage, allow for different approaches and constructions of spatial boundaries, for new forms of contact and exchange, for new forms of learning, and thus altering conceptual boundaries (Van Assche and Hornidge 2014).

In the case of Sulina, social boundaries shifted since many groups disappeared or shrank, and others, such as the Russian and Ukrainian speaking groups, changed their narratives and thus boundaries dramatically. We will talk more about these ethnic-cultural definitions in the following chapters. Here, we emphasize the importance of changing spatial boundaries, with first of all the stabilization of the lower Danube under the CED, as a spatial unity under unitary control, and later the importance of the Romanian state and the European Union. Indeed, the Lower

6.4 New Borders and Boundaries

Danube only became something, a unity existing in policy and experience, in history and organization, in the period of the Crimean wars, when the area became a problem for Western Europe (Rosetti et al. 2006[1931]; Sherman 1923). One can speak of a conceptual object, in European politics and media, that resulted from a conflict, from a simmering issue that now erupted, an issue that came with a weakening Ottoman Empire, a strong Russian Empire, and a European interest in the region (cf Duineveld et al. 2013). The now defunct Habsburg Empire identified with the Danube, making its lower reaches important, and there was, as said, an English interest in wheat from the Black Sea region. The conflict spawned the object, a conceptual boundary, which became a spatial boundary after the establishment of the CED and its control over Sulina, Tulcea, Galati, Braila. The minorities mentioned before had some presence already in these cities, and formed starting points for a densification and expansion of networks. In the CED era, the 'Danube Delta' was not a relevant concept, and did not come with relevant spatial boundaries. The Lower Danube was the area discussed everywhere and now controlled and redeveloped by the CED (Van Assche et al. 2012). People in Europe knew about it, and this made it interesting and gave a sense of unity in the area itself. As said, CED rule built on and encouraged existing forms of diversity, but did not intend to erase cultural or ethnic boundaries at all (Teampău and Van Assche 2009b).

As its territory and level of control shrank, the CED lost defining power of spatial boundaries, and the Danube Delta became slowly a spatial unit, again in a problematic sense, as resistance against communist development, as test case, in physical and cultural sense. Within the area itself, however, that unity was still not perceived, and locals spoke of their village, the regional town, and of the 'balta', the undifferentiated marshlands surrounding their village. Only with the founding of the Biosphere Reservation, and the institutional exception mentioned before, the assumption by the Reserve Administration of the role of regional government, did it dawn on many locals that 'the Danube Delta' was actually something. It was a unity coming with a conservationist perspective imposed by foreign actors and abused by regional ones-in their view. Research into the Delta, plans and policies for the Delta, restrictions in land and resource use because of the Delta. These things made the Delta alive and contested. Once again, the boundary came together with a conflict. People now are from the Delta, not only from their village, while the linkages with group definitions, with social boundaries, further erode.

The Danube delta is now a border of the EU, and narratives of all sorts converge upon this new boundary, narratives of ethnicity, of pasts and futures associated with groups, and with political entities existing and lost (Teampău and Van Assche 2007a, b). We mentioned the border police before. The new boundary is the old boundary, in place, but not in effects. It relates differently to social and conceptual boundaries, it reshapes groups by blocking old contacts, by reminding them of hopes of Europe all the time (we are in now, there is the border), but also by reminding them of an internal marginality (we are in but not in). Lipovans could be Russians when relations with Russia or the USSR where ok, not when they became problematic. Cossacks could be proud of the epithet when they were important or at least accepted, when network s connected them to other Cossacks (Subtelny 2009). The EU boundary brings a new scale into local games and narratives, a new set of narratives of Europe, and new effects of these narratives on networks and identifications (Van Assche and Hornidge 2014; Jacobs and Van Assche 2014). A EU border is defended differently, and a European identification brings European histories, policies, international relations, internal opportunities into focus. The new spatial boundary presents an additional force of reinterpretation of social and conceptual boundaries, directly, and indirectly, by enabling new movements, encounters and learning opportunities.

A spatial boundary which remained in place since the War, but changed meaning significantly, is the Romanian border. As a source of identification and as an actor, Romania had many faces in Sulina and the Danube Delta. As we know, for the Romanian state, CED control was a problem early on, yet also a form of protection they could use but were not ready to acknowledge. Once the state was more consolidated internally and backed up militarily and diplomatically on the international scene, it could afford to lose the CED, and worked on it through various channels. After the surrounding region, Dobrogea, was incorporated, the minorities that stood for the international character of also Sulina were disenfranchised, and not treated as full citizens of Romania (Iordachi 2002). After Sulina was incorporated, many people left, networks fragmented, and the balance of power shifted because Romania was for the Romanians, and because this suddenly became a border area (Van Assche et al. 2008). It had to be guarded, if necessary oppressed, since one could not trust the 'minorities' there, and, it would be best to redevelop and reinvent it (Verdery 1991; Boia 2001). New industries, forced migration, and attempts at land reclamation fit this grand strategy. With the arrival of the EU, and the disappearance of perceived threats locally, the state could again safely see the old diversity as an asset, an asset that could be sold to the EU, and for tourism. Also locally, EU membership resonated with old narratives, and the EU was seen as the new CED, bringing back the ships with gold and the hustle and bustle to the port. People openly speak of a new free port, a 'porto franco'.

References

Albert M, Jacobson D, Lapid Y (eds) (2001) Identities, borders, orders: rethinking international relations theory. University of Minnesota Press, Minneapolis
Allon F (2004) The consumption and construction of tourist spaces and landscapes in Sydney. Space Cult 7(1):49–63
Anderson B (1982) Imagined communities. Verso, London
Ascherson N (2007) The black sea: the birthplace of civilisation and barbarism. Random House, New York
Bart J (2004) Europolis. Bucuresti (1st edn, 1933)
Bélanger A (2000) Urban space and collective memory: analysing the various dimensions of the production of memory. Can J Urban Res 11(1):69–92
Bird SE (2002) It makes sense to us. Cultural identity in local legends of place. Contemp Ethnography 31(5):519–547

References

Boia L (2001) History and myth in Romanian consciousness. Central European University Press, Hungary

Duineveld M, Van Assche K, Beunen R (2013) Making things irreversible. Object stabilization in urban planning and design. Geoforum 46:16–24

Esposito E (2002) Soziales Vergessen: Formen und Medien des Gedachtnisses der Gesellschaft (Social forgetting: Form and medium in social memory). Suhrkamp, Frankfurt

Iordachi C (2002) Citizenship, nation-and state-building: the integration of Northern Dobrogea into Romania, 1878-1913. Carl Beck Pap Russ East Eur Stud 1607:86

Irwin-Zarecka I (1994) Frames of remembrance: the dynamics of collective memory. Transaction Books, New Brunswick

Jacobs J, Van Assche K (2014) Understanding empirical boundaries: a systems-theoretical avenue in border studies. Geopolitics 19(1):182–205

Judt T (2007) Postwar: a history of Europe since 1945. Pimlico, London

King C (2004) The black sea: a history. Oxford University Press, Oxford

Luhmann N (1995) Social systems. Stanford University Press, Stanford

Magris C (1988[1986]) Donau. Bert Bakker, Amsterdam

Mihailescu M, Vulpe R (1940) Dobrogea (Rumanian Academy. Romanian Studies IV). Imprimeria Nationala, Bucharest

Rosetti C et al (2006[1931]) La commission Europeenne du Danube et son oeuvre, de 1856–1931. Imprimerie Nationale, Paris

Sherman GE (1923) The international organization of the danube under the peace treaties. Am J Int Law 17(3):438–459

Simonsen K (2008) Practice, narrative and the multicultural city: a Copenhagen case. Eur Urban Reg Stud 15:145

Smith G (ed) (1998) Nation-building in the post-Soviet borderlands: the politics of national identities. Cambridge University Press, Cambridge

Stricker G (1990) Old believers in the territory of the Russian empire∗. Relig State Soc Keston J 18(1):25–51

Subtelny O (2009) Ukraine: a history. University of Toronto Press, Toronto

Teampău P (2009) Sulina—oraşul de la capătul lumii. In: Cuceu I (ed) Alternative antropologice şi etnologice în cercetarea culturilor. Studii şi comunicări. EFES, Cluj, pp 339–350

Teampău P (2010) Sulina traita de Panait Zachis. EFES, Cluj

Teampău P (2011) Sulina, alta lume, alta viata. EFES, Cluj

Teampău P (2013) Sulina fabuloasa. EFES, Cluj

Teampău P, Van Assche K (2007a) Sulina, the dying city in a vital region: social memory and the nostalgia for a European future. Ethnologia Balkanica 13(1):257–278

Teampău P, Van Assche K (2007b) Sulina, the dying city in a vital region. Social memory and nostalgia for the European future. Ethnologia Balkanica 11(1):257–278

Teampău P, Van Assche K (2009a) Migratory marginalities: making sense of home, self and mobility. Ethnologia Balkanica 13:147–163

Teampău P, Van Assche K (2009b) Sulina, Sulina, when there's water, there's no light. Memory and autobiography in a Romanian town, Identities. J Politics Gend Cult 7(1–2):33–70

Van Assche K (2004) Signs in time. An interpretive account of urban planning and design, the people and their histories. Wageningen University, Wageningen

Van Assche K, Hornidge AK (2014) Hidden mobilities in post-soviet spaces. Boundaries, scales, identities and informal routes to livelihood. Crossroads Asia Working Paper Series, 20

Van Assche K, Teampău P (2009) Layered encounters. Urban palimpsest and the performance of multiculturalism in the Romanian Danube Delta. Anthropol East Europe Rev 27(1):7–19

Van Assche K, Teampău P (2010) Landscape of the year. Social systems theory and the study of cultural and ecological adaptation in the Romanian Danube Delta. Studia Politica 15(1):83–102

Van Assche K, Teampău P, Devlieger P, Suciu C (2008) Liquid boundaries in marginal marshes. Reconstructions of identity in the Romanian Danube Delta. Studia Sociologia 39(1):115–138

Van Assche K, Devlieger P, Teampău P, Verschraegen G (2009) Remembering and forgetting in the margin: constructing past and future in the Romanian Danube Delta. Mem Stud 2(2):211–234

Van Assche K, Duineveld M, Beunen R, Teampău P (2011a) Delineating locals. Transformations of knowledge/power and the governance of the Danube Delta. J Environ Planning Policy Manage 13(1):1–21

Van Assche K, Beunen R, Jacobs J, Teampău P (2011b) Crossing trails in the marshes. Flexibility and rigidity in the governance of the Danube Delta. J Environ Plann Manage 54(8):997–1018

Van Assche K, Bell S, Teampău P (2012) Traumatic natures in the swamp. Concepts of nature and participatory governance in the Danube Delta. Environ Values 21(2):163–183

Van Assche K, Shtaltovna A, Hornidge A-K (2013) Visible and invisible informalities and institutional transformation. Lessons from transition countries: Georgia, Romania, Uzbekistan. In: Hayoz N, Giordano C (eds) Informality and post-socialist transition. Peter Lang, Frankfurt

Van Houtum H, Van Naerssen T (2002) Bordering, ordering and othering. Tijdschrift voor economische en sociale geografie 93(2):125–136

Verdery K (1991) National ideology under socialism: identity and cultural politics in Ceausescu's Romania. University of California Press, Berkeley

Chapter 7
Identities on the Move

Abstract In this chapter, we dwell on some of the more ambiguous and fluid phenomena in identity construction and place making encountered in Sulina, phenomena rendering the conceptualization of local cosmopolitanism more complex, because of the blurring of boundaries implied. We discuss migration and the way its renders fluid identities, of people and places, yet offers new sources of reinvention as well. Identity is then looked at through the prism of performance, and finally we discuss the impact of vanished groups and vanished places, because people left, or because the particular perspective of an assimilated group disappeared, while places can disappear literally, or from the narrative horizon of the community. Such absences can make reinvention in narrative easier, especially narratives about a cosmopolitan past, and attempts to reorient oneself to those narratives in the present.

Keywords Ambiguity · Identity · Migration · Reinvention · Mobilities · Social memory · Absence · Ethnicity · Silence · Performance · Multiculturalism

7.1 Fluid Identities and Migration

We already mentioned the narrative dynamics affecting identity construction, the rapid reconstruction of some ethnic categories. Other ethnic categories were able to absorb many people, and the Romanization process affected both groups already living there and people coming into work. The nature of old migration, i.e., escape, younger in-migration, often forced, and recent migration, which is largely out-migration, put specific pressures on the constructions of self and place in Sulina.

The functioning of local cosmopolitanism in Sulina, we believe, has to be understood against that background: a narrative of nostalgia and hope, associated with diversity, international networks and wealth, as a counterpoise for less pleasant memories and half-memories of waves of migration that were not well recorded, that were often traumatic for the migrants themselves and met with suspicion by regional authorities—since local authorities often did barely exist. The buffer character of the Danube Delta, positively appreciated by various empires, a character of a border zone, emphasizing zone over line, was ambiguous from the start, since people moved in and out of this porous swamp (Ascherson 1995). The Delta was hard to tame and conquer and bring into cultivation, but for individuals it was easily permeable. There are many access points, small boats bring you far, even before communist interventions there were many canals and small river branches to move around, higher river levees, islands and sand bars allowing for slow access over land as well, and opportunities to settle for small groups (Van Assche et al. 2008; Van Assche and Teampău 2010). Rules were hard to impose but people were moving. Harsh conditions thus combined with government suspicion, and the fragmentary social memory discussed before, to produce a situation in which ethnic pride and pride of place were hard to maintain. Sulina and its easily mythologized past help to balance the story (cf. Boia 2001) (Fig. 7.1).

After communism, economic opportunities were few and far between locally, and hit-and-run strategies or migration often proved the only way to survive. While things have improved since the nineties, times are still tough. Other than tourism, not much is going on, and, consequently, the hopes for tourism are high (Van Assche et al. 2009). Many people hoping for more tourism, and many people active in tourism, are aware of the past grandeur of Sulina, its prosperity, its rich cultural life, its international newspapers, its name and fame all over Europe.

Sulina, despite its modest size, and the limited time-frame that saw its development, is many things to many people. Even for long-time residents, it is not always easy which narrative to pick from in relating themselves to the place and its history. A unique cosmopolitan past is one of the reasons, a marginal position a second reason, a reinvention of the surroundings as 'nature' a third one (Van Assche et al. 2012). We argue that much of the confusion in the game of memories and counter-memories can be ascribed to the fact that these factors triggered a series of transformations that are volatile and far-reaching (Teampău and Van Assche 2009b). What appears to be a dormant village, deprived of economic assets, is reinventing itself continuously, in complex patterns, because of everything mentioned before, the depth of the conceptual transformations being increased by the same economic deprivation. In other words, a small, poor place, with a rich history that relates uneasily to the present inhabitants, and a naturalized physical environment that is perceived as alienated, is trying different versions of itself, in the performance of quickly shifting narratives.

Even with the pride taken in a cosmopolitan past, many young people do not see a future in Sulina or the delta (Van Assche et al. 2012). They move or want to move, and in some cases they want to come back to revive some of the old qualities lost now in Sulina, to contribute to its renaissance (Teampău and Van Assche 2009a, b). At the same time, surviving elsewhere, in the Europe that was perceived as golden in local narratives, often proves hard. Coming back is an option, and retelling stories about the golden past because of 'Europe', in the hope that Europe comes back, becomes less believable, more fraught with contradiction. Young people with positive migration experiences leave rarely a trace in Sulina, while those

7.1 Fluid Identities and Migration

Fig. 7.1 Sulina, Street II. You can see in the back the old lighthouse (still standing today) and the minaret of the Turkish mosque (disappeared after WWI) [Public domain]

who come back cannot sustain the same nostalgia. They cannot match up their stories of golden Sulina and golden Europe with what they experienced. For them, Sulina offers at least a place where they have social networks, where they can survive with no money, which is tougher even in other regions in Romania (Van Assche and Teampău 2009). Starting a business in Sulina proves harder, because of local competition and resentment, because of locally entrenched interests and corruption, and because the link between local and regional networks is tenuous too. Finding a bank in a regional center to support an investment in Sulina is tough.

The formerly cosmopolitan character of Sulina presents another obstacle to coming back, reinvesting and reviving the cosmopolitan dream: ownership. As said, many people left Sulina over the decades, including the merchant minorities. During communism, properties were collectivized, and after communism the task of privatization became daunting in Sulina, because tracing the rightful owners, the closest relatives of former owners, can take years, and does not always lead to a clear and clean resolution. The current owners of a single home in Sulina can be scattered over several countries, might not be aware of their ownership, might not agree on a proper strategy and might not even be interested in seeing the place, while they also do not want to sell. Redevelopment or renovation is tough under those conditions. Eminent domain could be a solution but reminds locals too much of a powerful government communist style (Van Assche et al. 2011a). History ties down the present, and prevents the survival and economic re-appropriation of the CED past (Van Assche et al. 2011b). The complex nature and the currently fragmented and ruptured character of the old networks that supported Sulina, create many obstacles for a practicable revival of a local cosmopolitanism.

The emphasis on nature conservation in the surrounding Danube Delta, the peculiar role of the Biosphere reserve administration in regional governance, the official emphasis on sustainable development, in fact on non-development, increases the pressure to migrate since few see other options. The overly strict character of formal rules of development only increases the important of informal rules, of clans, networks, corruption, and of a closure in governance, a lack of participation and inclusion (Van Assche et al. 2013). Even within the old fishing profession, options are fewer than before, since the government introduced a lease system for the fishing grounds in the Delta, de facto offering large concessions to well connected businessmen and reducing the fishermen to either criminals or employees of these concessionaires (Van Assche et al. 2011a). This structural reduction of the options for young people fuels the imagination of old Europe and the CED and the imagination of greener pastures beyond the horizon. Europe old and new are again connected through the tropes of CED Sulina. Sulina in this discourse was a place of freedom, freedom to do business, choose a profession (Teampău and Van Assche 2007).

Also those who did not move and are not planning to move, see new faces and new interpretations of Europe, some years after accession (2007). This, in turn, leads to a new step in the reshuffling of narratives of identity, of past and future, and a reconstruction of local cosmopolitanism. The tourists who do show up are not the ones seen on American TV series, and not the ones remembered from

7.1 Fluid Identities and Migration 91

communist times. Indeed, also the communist economic development approach to the Delta included tourism, a sort of eco tourism avant la lettre, focused on catching and eating fish, while enjoying a beer with friends. Fishing is still popular with Romanian tourists, who never forgot the place (cf. Panighiant 1972), but there is an awareness that foreign tourists bring more money, and that those are generally interested in nature, in 'the Delta', more than Sulina. Resentment is one response, adaptation another one (Van Assche and Teampău 2010). In the same conversation, one can encounter a scorching critique of the Biosphere reserve administration and its exclusion of locals in decision-making, its blind emphasis on green goals and its blind eye towards those who claim to be green but are not, and, a few minutes later, a declaration of love to 'nature', to the beauties of the Danube Delta, and to the potential of eco-tourism. Europe becomes seen as the power behind the green discourses that are strangling them, but at the same time comes with a message that money can be made by commodifying the environment (Van Assche et al. 2012). Old enemies turn into enemies of the environment, and one can align oneself quickly with green goals, provided they offer space for local entrepreneurship.

Migration can look different every few minutes in such conversations, and the constructions of self and place, of the linkages between them, can alter in the same time span (Teampău and Van Assche 2009a; Van Assche and Hornidge 2014). One minute no other options than migration are perceived, the next one can envision a way to stay there, capitalize on an environment that now becomes a resource, an asset in a new way, beyond fish. As we mentioned before, in Sulina, local identity is largely underlined by recurrent narratives of piracy and cosmopolitanism, by taking pride in breaking the laws of a center one does not identify with. The often-quoted local saying "we are the first to see the sun and the last to see justice" expresses a deeply felt marginality, both geographical and political. Sulina, as the former seat of the European Danube Committee (CED) boasts of a history of international connections and local ethnic diversity ["*My mother had nine first cousins in Paris*"]. Thus, for the people of Sulina, Europe represents a return and a re-placement, but also, like for any other Eastern Europeans, the glamour and the lure of a better life, and the locus of preconceived concepts (democracy, freedom, good life etc.) (Teampău and Van Assche 2009a: 155).

We have described, elsewhere (Teampău and Van Assche 2009a) the cases of two migrants from Sulina illustrating one way or another not only the emblematic stories of migration but also the specificity of drifting and returning to a place like Sulina. For C., one of our characters, Europe enjoys a special imaginary: he still preserves from his childhood during communism the image of the golden fishing hooks of the German tourists, glittering in the sun, as opposed to the ugly darkbrown Russian ones, easily breaking. For him, this image remained the essence of the glamor and glitter of Europe. In reality, post-experience, Europe came to mean a lifestyle he could not really agree with: *people are obsessed with money and live their life like looking through glass, as if you see what is happening through a glass, you do not feel what you are doing. While here in Sulina and in other isolated places you really feel life. You do not have the instruments to do what you want, but you improvise to make ends meet. In Europe they have everything, but do not know how to use it.* He seems to value this savoir-vivre, living life to extremes (even those of poverty). *When I came back, I felt in heaven, I was mastering my own life again, which I couldn't in Europe, where I did not know anyone.* C's story is a story of freedom, looking for a complete fulfillment of the self, which in the end can only be realized at home (Teampău and Van Assche 2009a: 155–156). The physical isolation of Sulina, separated by swamp, river and sea from the rest of the world, makes it easier to imagine it as a remote hell, and as a safe haven. The difference with the surroundings can easily be articulated, a territory can be easily staked out (Van Assche and Teampău 2010).

The marginality of Sulina drove C and S to migration, and it followed them every step along the way. Both C and S are keenly aware of the limitations and the lure of Sulina: 'man, look at this place!' and 'damn, what are we doing here' oscillate in an affective equilibrium that is highly unstable. The same oscillation is a continuous questioning of self, a continuous confrontation with the possibilities and the threats of an open identity. Sulina, 'at the end of the world', allows them to reinvent themselves freely, to toy semi-ironically with various labels for identification ('artist', 'fisherman', 'traveller', 'businessman'), but its marginality also creates obstacles for careers in any of the designated fields. Creating a home by choosing a profession and adopting a relatively stable identity is therefore very hard, and Sulina pushes and pulls men like a film noir *femme fatale* (Teampău and Van Assche 2009a: 159). Europe imagined at home, in the cosmopolitan atmosphere of narrative Sulina, projected as "familiar", as part of one's development, proved quite different to the "real" Europe of the unwanted migrant.

During communism, life was defined by specific agendas in Sulina. As one informant reports, because people had, most of them similar incomes and similar ways of life, they found it easier to live together as a community, without major tensions. *"We also lived as a community because, except for summer, we lived among ourselves, like a family. Once the tourists, the guests, were gone, we were the same family again. Also, we went to Tulcea with the ship "The Passenger" where you could meet anyone; it was a connector to the outside world. But there was also another strange thing: you could see so many ships passing, right under your nose, with different flags, coming and going, and still you couldn't leave. That was frustrating. Even for sailors it was difficult: for maritime sailors there was a special approval required from the authorities"* (Teampău 2013: 144). After the 1989 revolution and the fall of communism, people in Sulina felt less and less isolated, and with the emergence of internet connections, even less. Sulina is still physically isolated; it can only be reached by boat from Tulcea, but occasionally, during the summer touristic season, it can become crowded. *"Tourists are rather good for Sulina; you need to take contact with other people, to exchange ideas. Most of them are a universe in themselves, and you interact and learn new things. I remember a few summers in which tourists did not come, for different reasons, and then the city was acutely empty during the summer. It was one of the saddest summers ever"* (Teampău 2013: 154). In fact, Sulina lives in two different life rhythms, determined by the summer season and the off-season intimacy of the "family".

7.2 Performance of Multiculturalism and Urban Space

Ethnic and cultural boundaries are both reinforced and undermined in the present field of forces affecting Sulina. Commodification for tourism and within a nation state turning more sensitive to multiculturalism reinforces boundaries, while unraveling local networks, schools, memory mechanisms, and homogenizing forces of Romania and Europe contribute to their undermining.

One can surmise though, that in all periods, including the CED period, people resorted to different identity narratives on different occasions. The unifying narrative of 'Sulina' seems to be of relatively recent origin, but with precursors under the CED, when the place was promoted as a proof of the success of the CED regime. The unifying narrative however has many shades and offers space for the performance of multiculturalism in many guises. One can speak of a taking up, sometimes explicitly, sometimes implicitly, of different roles, associated with different narratives of self and Sulina, for different occasions.

Cultural festivals offer occasions to highlight an ethnic identity, religious services, family feasts and gatherings, but also new visitors, new projects invoking a multicultural past or present, and new discussion in general about opening up governance at the local or regional level. Forgotten identities can be revived, and some people who do not identify as Russian or Old Believer are still labeled as such by other older people in the town. The current large group of Old Believers, a group who colonized Sulina from the margins, wavers between stories of old multiculturalism, old oppression, and current prominence (Van Assche et al. 2008, 2011a). The Greek minority is active and proud, but members shift without effort to Romanian identifications, or stories of pervasive hybridism. Mr. Zachis, the guardian of memory mentioned before, remembers different ethnic versions of CED Sulina, emphasizing sometimes more the unity in diversity, sometimes more the diversity, in other cases the hierarchies in place (with Western Europeans at the top, above the merchant minorities, while Old Believers and Romanians did the tough job). The phrase 'We're all Romanian now' can be invoked at any time to smoothen out differences discussed just before (Teampău 2010).

One cannot always speak of strategy and clear cut 'occasions' asking for strategic identification (Van Assche and Teampău 2009). In many cases, the memories of past identities and hybrids are not clear, the image of a collective past is not clear, and the fit between them cannot be assessed easily. Often, there are fragments of stories of place, self and group which do not fit the standard Romanian school book, nor the standard phrases about CED Sulina, small eruptions of alternatives, of old variations, old connections, distinctions and performances. If there is reflection on this different tapestry of actions and stories, this slightly different performance of self in this environment, a special character of place is invoked, possibly followed by a repetition of the standard story, without reflecting on the inconsistency between that story and the more subtle traces of a more complex past which just asserted itself (Teampău and Van Assche 2009b). 'Multiculturalism' is a new label and a new commodity in this ongoing performance. We already mentioned that the actual lineage of people is not the only factor in understanding these traces of the past; the stories subsume new people in the character of place (Hinchman and Hinchman 1997). This shows itself in explicit identifications and retellings, and it shows itself in subtle practical adaptations, in different turns of speech, different relations between people, different assessments of the environment, what is possible and appropriate. Newcomers became immersed in the past of Sulina, in a set of narratives that shaped and modulated behavior beyond narrative performance.

Now few people speak more than two languages and non-Romanian languages are largely confined to private spaces or one neighborhood which is the liminal zone between city and swamp, where Sulina fades into a narrow strip of higher land, a Lipoveni neighborhood. The dominance of Romanian operates as a sign of unity and practices at a different level a nationalist unity also reinforced under communism. However, other languages are still there, and do present barriers. Minority languages are signs of otherness that cannot be completely reinterpreted under the banner of cosmopolitanism. Under the CED people probably did not speak 4–5 languages, except for the multilingual CED-administration to which their archives bear witness and some of the more cosmopolitan merchants (who had at the very least a working knowledge of the languages of various customers). Yet many people did speak more languages than they do today while the fluidity and complexity of group boundaries was clearly greater (cf. Van Assche and Teampău 2009: 14). As one old lady recalls: "most people in Sulina spoke at least three languages: Greek, Russian and Romanian. In our house my parents used to talk Romanian to us and Greek to each other; Greek was the language of secrets. Our parents knew Greek better than Romanian. My grandfather on my mother side also spoke fluently Turkish. I remember he met in Tulcea a Turk guy and spoke to him; until then, I had no idea that he could speak Turkish" (Teampău 2013: 33).

A factor rendering the tapestry more complex is distrust. Trust was a scarce good in communist Europe, it is a scarce good in marginal communities, and it is scarce where networks are reshuffled all the time (Verdery 1991; Boia 2001). Distrust and suspicion show themselves in allegations of witchcraft, sorcery, of corruption, shady pasts and shady affiliations. Since the waves of people coming from the villages to the city during communism, the deeper composition of Sulina changed: people brought with them habits and rituals from the countryside, which shimmer through the thin layer of urbanity. Mostly in the margins of Sulina, but not only, one can see the skull of a horse "protecting" a gate from evil spirits, or can notice people avoiding some spots on the streets or crossing themselves when passing certain corners. The dark side of Sulina is not easily perceptible, but it is present in all kinds of stories and urban legends about ghosts, suicides or curses.

Even barely distinguishable groups can become the bearers of suspicion. A Lipovan identity can be irrelevant one moment for the interlocutors, but later remembered and invoked when a conflict, a jealousy, a tension shows up and has to be explained or reproduced. Religious tolerance can similarly be practiced and preached, while traces of distrust linger on in the shades, and the other religions are quietly compared with witchcraft, oracle and magic (Van Assche et al. 2012). Distrust can modify the perception of self and other, and induce different behaviors and

7.2 Performance of Multiculturalism and Urban Space

interpretations of place. The special Sulina of one moment is a cauldron of conflicts and resentment later. Complexity brings confusion, and confusion in this case can be tolerated because the value of modulations in the fabric of identity is not very high. The stakes are not high, the assets to compete over are not accessible anyway to those competing locally, and the local networks that do come with benefits, are marked more by communist ties than ethnic or cultural features. A multiplicity of readings of self and place remains possible, and what is inconsistent does not disrupt the multiplicity, the actual balance of power, and the actual networks (cf. Van Assche et al. 2008).

Urban places, as dynamic contexts of social interaction and memory, are not only ideology-informed, but have the power to coalesce and sustain a community. Fluid and unsettled, places are never innocent settings, but political stakes of symbolic (and physical) appropriation. Suffused with meaning, laden with memories, the urban landscape can provide a suitable apparatus for anchoring processes of remembering. Moreover, even though memory evokes itself in urban settings through space, those particular places that memory "revives", "remembers", do not have to necessarily exist (or have existed). Memory can work with absences, too. Absence can sometimes manufacture a more powerful evocative effect (Mills 2006; Van Assche and Costaglioli 2012).

Urban space, its signs of the past, of old distinctions and practices, offers a frame of reference and a landscape of opportunities for such performances, of culture and of multiculturalism. Performances can be fully conscious, or not. They can be object of strategy, or not. They can be blended, or not. The intended audience for the performance can be singular or multiple, it can be present or absent (Van Assche and Teampău 2009). The mere existence of this old urban space in this unexpected environment, surrounded by sea and vast marshes, inhabited by people barely remembering why they're there and why this place was built, cannot but provoke reflection and influence identification. All are aware of the uniqueness of the place, and the built environment immediately invokes questions about the past, about foreign connections, about an old diversity and prosperity (Teampău and Van Assche 2009a). The gradual decrease of urban character away from the waterfront, in the space of four or five blocks, the grid pattern of streets, the larger landmark buildings, water tower, light house, CED head quarters, all remind inhabitants and tourists of a very different past, inspire hopes for the future and force locals to locate themselves again. As said, the absence of strong local memories and of strong social memory of the more recent immigrants, of attractive identifications, inserts a productive flexibility in the identity narratives. One can change oneself and change the place identity at the same time, and few will contest it (Van Assche 2004; Hinchman and Hinchman 1997).

One can see the urban space as a palimpsest, not in the sense that several layers of meaning are waiting to be read or discovered, but in the sense of a matrix, offering a potential for different readings, for different performances of culture and multi-culture (Van Assche et al. 2008). What is there, the materiality of urban space, the contrast with the surrounding physical landscape, lends itself to an interpretation as a space of exception, a privileged place, a glorious past, a cultured past. It lends itself to a re-enactment of these glories, of the associated identities, but also to a reflection on the world at large of which this past town was a privileged part. The material surroundings do not impose but provoke ideas of the world at large asserting itself here, to the paradox of privileged access to and representation of the world as such, at least the developed world, in this marginal place. The contrast between town and landscape entangles with the contrast between central past and marginal present, and reinforces the paradox of the center in the margin, the presence of the whole in the most unexpected part (cf. Deleuze and Guattari 1987).

Such Deleuzian version of the palimpsest comes close to the concept of rhizome, but one which can be navigated and activated, one which is open to human agency. Vanished networks and loss of narrative connectivity make certain versions of the matrix less likely than others, less actively virtual, yet the urban fabric, the reproduction and reinvention of place, history and identity narratives still structure the productivity of the matrix, in the sense of enabling and delimiting. A house can be Armenian or Greek, but not Turkish; a swamp is not a canal; a Greek can speak Romanian but probably not Russian, a Lipovan can be atheist but probably not Muslim; peaceful coexistence can be undermined in silence, but multiculturalism cannot be combined with street fights. Old links with Paris can be easily claimed, but present ignorance of Paris cannot easily be disguised. People, places, occasions, can trigger shifts in the matrix, can bring other layers, other interpretations to the fore.

7.3 Vanished Groups and Their Narrative Impact

Cosmopolitanism in Sulina relies on and refers to groups that are either gone or almost gone, and when they are still here, they are Romanized in many ways. The old networks are gone, the old institutions and organizations to reproduce the old identity, the archive and much of the living memory. As others have pointed out, it is easier to be a multicultural place when the others are left. It is easier to have a cosmopolitan past than present, in that sense. The difficulties to negotiate difference in daily life, are gone. It is easier to forget those, and to remold the identities of others, and their modes of coexistence, after the cultural fabric has been simplified (Mills 2006; Van Assche 2004). Difference is still acknowledged, but either for tourism, or in the manner of socialist folklore, where 'minorities' were marked by innocent dances, dishes and customs, without affecting power/knowledge configurations vital to the state.

Since groups are gone or have changed beyond recognition compared to the CED days, their frames of references, their modes of observation and their memory functions cannot be fully understood and reconstructed (Van Assche et al. 2009; cf. Luhmann 1995). Moreover, they do not play a role in the everyday reproduction of local cosmopolitanism. Their absence has an impact in the sense of creating narrative freedom for the others to reinvent their image and the image of the place. They can also have 'positive' narrative legacies, starting with the fact that they are remembered (Zarecka 1994). We distinguish between absence, presence and non-existence, where a present absence is positively noted, whereas a past absence, a never-presence, is interpreted as non-existence (Felder et al. 2014). Non-existence is non-existence in discourse, meaning that something or someone could have been there, but without leaving discursive trails and traces. Absence will spark discursive responses, as a result of comparison to another known state. It can trigger reflection on the reason of absence, on the change taken place, on shifting identities. Non-existence can stem from an actual non-existence, and it can come from what we call deep forgetting, a forgetting of forgetting, a loss of the conditions of remembering (cf. Hinchman and Hinchman 1997).

When the frames of discourse which allowed for certain memory selections are gone, also disappeared, bringing back the memory is nearly impossible. This deep forgetting is different from the normal forgetting, where remembering afterwards is also more than recall, is also a new selection of concepts tinged by a current situation. With deep forgetting, the perspectives which created something and/or the perspectives and infrastructures which enabled transmitting (i.e., reinterpretation, transformation) of certain semantics, are gone. People, as social groups, represent such perspectives. Whereas the perspectives of vanished Armenians can never be captured, those who are not remembered leave no narrative traces. Their actual networked existence, their contribution through connectivity to local cosmopolitanism, will not be grasped at all and will not be susceptible at all to understanding, to recreation, or to replacement by an equivalent form of connectivity.

We would argue that the history of marginality in the Delta contributed to deep forgetting (Van Assche et al. 2009). The unstable social memories and physical landscapes of the marshlands, the fishermen moving to a largely abandoned Sulina, enrolling in narratives of cosmopolitanism, all this is not conducive to an understanding of old Sulina, how it works, what the cosmopolitanism rested upon. We know by now that the situation afforded great narrative flexibility, but it also brought severe restrictions to memory; it favored deep forgetting. Deep forgetting, we will argue, causes problems for coordination, for policy-making, for development, as old forms of coordination, old networks are forgotten and futures are envisioned which rest on fantasies which are hard to pin down.

Just like many people in the villages rewrote their history and identity, reducing it to a simple narrative of marginality, so the people from Sulina, mostly coming from the villages, rewrote their identities, downplayed ethnic boundaries, and inscribed themselves in the multicultural and international identity of Sulina. Even when any centrality in political, cultural, economic sense is long gone, this identity of place still survives, succeeds in adopting new people, redefining them, turning them into Sulinese. The histories of Sulina used in this process were originally largely the histories of people now gone, but they are simplified and revived constantly (cf. Van Assche et al. 2008: 129).

Absent people are more easily transformed into types, positive or negative, and the places they marked, if recognized, can structure narratives of Sulina (Mills 2006; Magris 2011). It is also possible that narratives rooted in stories of a group now gone, provide structures and elements of current narratives, whether this is remembered or not. People leave, stories survive, not only about them, but also told by them. The link between story and vanished storyteller is not always remembered. One can include here the CED bureaucracy and their self-promotion: this seems to have left a mark on the positive stories of wealth and coexistence under the European flag, driven by trade and accompanied by strong bureaucratic planning. The CED was active at several levels in its self-promotion: locally, regionally, and internationally, where it transcended its initial mandate, and made itself more important and enduring thanks to its development-orientation.

The 'oriental' aspects of some vanished groups have disappeared from the narratives. 'The Greeks', the 'Jews', the 'Armenians' are now associated with types in local stories and with nation states secondarily (Teampău and Van Assche 2009b). Their function in CED Sulina, as brokers and mediators of western and eastern networks, is not visible in the local cosmopolitanism of today (Teampău 2011, 2013). It seems clear that the CED-era versions of local cosmopolitanism were much more tinged with elements that were and would not be recognized as European today. One has to add that each of these three groups, Jews, Armenians and Greeks, were present in complex networks of rather cosmopolitan places, each maintaining many interactions with other groups, but also maintaining a cultural identity and community that can be described as cosmopolitan *in themselves*.

These ethnic-commercial networks operated on the basis of a few shared features, and they could accommodate substantial internal difference; Jewish, Greek or Armenian people could come from communities far away, bring different foods, customs and languages, but as long as they were recognized as belonging, trade and interaction, and mutual support, could continue (Ascherson 1995). Jewish dishes could differ around the Mediterranean and Black Seas, Jewish people could be familiar with these places and dishes, and Jewish dishes could betray the travels of people and communities across regions. Armenian groups could re-label as Hungarian, in some Romanian cities where they could occupy a functionally equivalent position and were welcomed. In these same Transylvanian communities, the 'Germans' or 'Saxons' would incorporate elements from diverse lineage, mostly Western-European though (Kann 1974). While the 'Greeks' of the Black and Mediterranean Seas, and especially in South Eastern Europe, would incorporate people from equally diverse provenance, as long as they cooperated in the same trade networks, could speak some Greek, and travel. (We do not touch here upon the Roma communities in the region, which at some time were highly organized in guilds, later turned into rest-categories at the bottom of the social ladder, where everyone could end up when things went wrong; Achim 2004.)

These communities, in their differently, more networked form of cosmopolitanism, and their different internal versions of *local* cosmopolitanism, have left little trace on the current forms and functions of local cosmopolitanism.

7.4 Vanished Places and Their Narrative Impact

Not only people disappear, also places. Vanished groups can alter narrative dynamics and network dynamics by virtue of their vanishing; while they can also leave traces of various sorts. The same is true for places.

We can distinguish between local places that vanished, in the sense of buildings demolished, or areas that are not recognizable anymore in their unity as associated

7.4 Vanished Places and Their Narrative Impact   99

with this or that group, and places farther away that disappeared behind the horizon. With new spatial and cultural boundaries asserting themselves, with shifting networks, either caused by or causing boundary shifts, perspectives change, narratives on self and place (Jacobs and Van Assche 2014; Van Assche and Hornidge 2014). But also places change, in their narrative construction and also, more elementary, in their visibility. Some places are still accessible but became invisible in local narratives, while others became less accessible because of new borders, or became less attractive to visit or to remember, because of shifting economic and cultural networks, or because of traumatic memories.

In the interwar period, when CED was still present (up until 1939), the city had the life of any other cosmopolitan flourishing harbor. As part of the general narrative of the "good old times," a Greek informant (Mrs. N., 75) remembers a Public Garden and the fanfare of the City Hall, with public performances every Sunday. "Ladies would wear long dresses, nice cloths, hats; there were stores with English and imported fabrics. On the second street was the shop of an Armenian seller. People were very elegant." Life in inter-war Sulina is painted in light colors (somehow blind to ethnic and class differences): "The Greeks organized very fancy balls, where people had to wear formal dress" (Obviously, the Lipoveni fishermen had no knowledge of such codes). All these details of a long-disappeared bourgeois world are mixed, in the case of Sulina, with traces of a multicultural prosperous urban life. "There was a café with cookies, a lemonade shop held by the Zamfiropol family, who were very secretive about its recipe. Another Armenian, Echmegean, had a lemonade-shop. Peasants came with food to the market: lots of yellow butter, flour". When our informant was a child (early '30s), Sulina was still very developed, a thriving harbor with cosmopolitan connections. "Many ships brought citric to the city and loaded grains here. The waterfront was full of ships loaded with wheat. This kind of commerce was in the hands of the Greeks. It was a very silent city; there was no dust because there was only one car in the city, belonging to an Armenian, Hurşud. My father was a harbor worker. Higher paid people working for the Commission were not locals. Jews, most of the Armenians and Greeks were involved in commerce, but the others were poor and less educated. There were few Lipovans in Sulina before the war" (cf. Teampău and Van Assche 2009a: 45–46).

"Greek" narratives have in common a certain impression of the antebellum life in Sulina, with emphasis on the commercial aspects and details of a day-to-day comfortable life. Mr. Zachis also remembers a similar urban landscape: "First Street was almost exclusively made up of shops, cafes, with apartments above, and over 80 % of the owners were Greeks, some Armenians, and Jews too. Every merchant in the city made a list of products they needed, brought to them every week by ship. The second street was one of residences mainly, with larger gardens. I remember everybody was supposed to dress nicely for Easter, in new clothes, so we went to Jewish textile sellers; they called the Armenian tailor, who was paid in advance by the textile sellers. People were reliable so as to buy on credit." (cf. Teampău and Van Assche 2009a: 47).

The recent communist past, although programmatically absent from the mainstream urban and social discourse, is everywhere present in the form of abandoned factories and blocks of flats, vacant "universal shops" or inscriptions on the walls. The ruins in the urban scenery of Sulina (old damaged houses, sometimes just a façade still standing while on the inside wild vegetation has literally consumed the walls, abandoned shops still bearing "communist" inscriptions) speak different memories and evoke different stories and ghosts. They make up a contradictory and heterogeneous urban landscape, with restaurants full of lights and voices neighboring a silent and dim empty house, the former communist market, deserted for years and suddenly transformed into the most fashionable open air restaurant for tourists, hiding behind it the unpretentious local taverns mostly frequented by Lipoveni.

In Sulina, the fish-tinning factory, built upon the place of a destroyed Armenian church, stands quiet in the sun, in a deceptive anonymity. A critical challenge for the researcher would be to unravel all those embodied, sensual memories which are still dormant or have been intentionally muted by prevailing narratives. In a place like Sulina, with so many overlapping semiotic and mnemonic layers, in which political and social features have changed the rules of the game, at least in surface, so many times, gaining access to such memories and minutiae of day-to-day life during communism, to the embodied memories of working in a factory and the biographical details of the transition from rural to (cvasi)urban living, would open up a new and deeper understanding of this particular place, of the stories people tell and the stories they hide, all of them, in one way or another, shaping the current life and landscape of Sulina.

Not only the Greeks used to function in a differently networked world in the 19th century; this also applies to the various Russian and Ukrainian speaking groups, whose histories are often hard to trace. Their links with the Don area, with communities in Ukraine and Bulgaria, are remembered by a few academics only. Only a few places close to the current border still figure in the living memory. If pressed, people might speak of 'the Bulgarians' here in the region, but very few remember that this was Bulgaria for a while, that this affected identification and movement of people. Few realize that the Greeks here could have close ties to the Ottomans, not only to Greece, furthermore that they could have relatives in the now Bulgarian port cities of Burgas and Sozopol and that their houses looked very similar, that they read about the same architectural fashions in Europe and a Europeanizing Istanbul (Ascherson 1995; King 2004). Sozopol, Istanbul, Athens are now beyond the horizon, and an acknowledged diversity does not include these places, their appearance, their connections and learning opportunities. The languages of the places are forgotten. The Jewish Ladino language, previously present on the lower Danube, e.g. in Ruse, where Elias Canetti grew up, speaking the language, is nearly dead, and Ruse itself is now Bulgaria (Magris 2011).

Places do not have perspectives that can be lost; they are not ways of seeing and remembering, as one can associate with groups. What they have in common is the capacity to affect narrative dynamics in the community by the act of vanishing, and by actively leaving traces (Jacobs and Van Assche 2014). Positive and negative mechanisms are hard to disentangle later, when places or groups are gone, precisely because of their disappearance. Stories about old networks, activities, old differences and similarities, ways to live together and share the wealth, can more easily be transformed when people and places are gone. As long as the story of their past importance remains believable locally, they can remain part of it, despite and thanks to their disappearance (Smith 1998).

An explicit link with anthropology offered by Massey (2005) is the presentation of places as evolving conglomerates of stories, all with their own rhythm and intensity, all potentially affecting each other, and anyone passing. Identity, as eternal change, as continuous aggregation and disaggregation of forces and series of events, will enter relations with places that can be conceived as formation of new stories, some short-lived, some with a longer lease in new contexts. Massey (2005, 189) qualifying spaces as 'multiplicities of stories-so-far', says elsewhere (175): "We are always, inevitably, making spaces and places. The temporary cohesions of articulations of relations, the provisional and partial enclosures, [...] these spatial forms are the necessary fixings of communication and identity".

References

Achim V (2004) The Roma in Romanian history. Kendall Hunt, London
Ascherson N (1995) Black Sea. 1st edn. University of Michigan Press, Ann Arbor
Boia L (2001) History and myth in Romanian consciousness. Central European University Press
Deleuze G, Guattari F (1987) A thousand plateaus. University of Minnesota Press, Minneapolis
Felder M, Duineveld M, Assche KV (2014) Absence/Presence and the ontological politics of heritage: the case of Barrack 57. Int J Heritage Stud (ahead-of-print) 1–16
Hinchman LP, Hinchman SK (eds) (1997) Memory, identity, community: the idea of narrative in the human sciences. SUNY Press
Jacobs J, Van Assche K (2014) Understanding empirical boundaries: a systems-theoretical avenue in border studies. Geopolitics 19(1):182–205
Kann RA (1974) A history of the Habsburg Empire, 1526–1918. University of California Press, Berkeley
King C (2004) The black sea: a history. Oxford University Press, Oxford
Luhmann N (1995) Social systems. Stanford University Press, Stanford
Magris C (2011) Danube. Random House, New York
Massey D (2005) For space. Sage, London
Mills A (2006) Boundaries of the nation in the space of the urban: landscape and social memory in Istanbul. Cult Geographies 13(3):367–394
Panighiant (1972) Le delta du Danube, Bucharest, Editions Touristiques
Smith G (ed) (1998) Nation-building in the post-Soviet borderlands: the politics of national identities. Cambridge University Press, Cambridge
Teampău P (2010) Sulina traita de Panait Zachis. EFES, Cluj
Teampău P (2011) Sulina, alta lume, alta viata. EFES, Cluj
Teampău P (2013) Sulina fabuloasa. EFES, Cluj
Teampău P, Van Assche K (2007) Sulina, the dying city in a vital region. Social memory and nostalgia for the European future. Ethnologia Balkanica 11(1):257–278
Teampău P, Van Assche K (2009a) Migratory marginalities: making sense of home, self and mobility. Ethnologia Balkanica 13:147–163
Teampău P, Van Assche K (2009b) Sulina, Sulina, when there's water, there's no light. Memory and autobiography in a Romanian town. Identities J Polit Gend Cult 7(1–2):33–70
Van Assche K (2004) Signs in time. An interpretive account of urban planning and design, the people and their histories. Wageningen University, Wageningen

Van Assche K, Costaglioli F (2012) Silent places, silent plans: Silent signification and the study of place transformation. Plann Theory 11(2):128–147

Van Assche K, Hornidge AK (2014) Hidden mobilities in post-Soviet Spaces. Boundaries, scales, identities and informal routes to livelihood. Crossroads Asia Working Paper Series, No. 20

Van Assche K, Teampău P (2009) Layered encounters. Urban palimpsest and the performance of multiculturalism in the Romanian Danube Delta. Anthropol East Europe Rev 27(1):7–19

Van Assche K, Teampău P (2010) Landscape of the year. Social systems theory and the study of cultural and ecological adaptation in the Romanian Danube delta. Studia Politica 15(1):83–102

Van Assche K, Teampău P, Devlieger P, Suciu C (2008) Liquid boundaries in marginal marshes. Reconstructions of identity in the Romanian Danube Delta. Studia Sociologia 39(1):115–138

Van Assche K, Devlieger P, Teampău P, Verschraegen G (2009) Remembering and forgetting in the margin: constructing past and future in the Romanian Danube Delta. Memory Stud 2(2):211–234

Van Assche K, Duineveld M, Beunen R, Teampău P (2011a) 'Delineating locals. Transformations of knowledge/power and the governance of the Danube delta. J Environ Policy Plann 13(1):1–21

Van Assche K, Beunen R, Jacobs J, Teampău P (2011b) Crossing trails in the marshes. Flexibility and rigidity in the governance of the Danube delta. J Environ Plann Manage 54(8):997–1018

Van Assche K, Bell S, Teampău P (2012) Traumatic natures in the swamp. Concepts of nature and participatory governance in the Danube delta. Environ Values 21(2):163–183

Van Assche K, Shtaltovna A, Hornidge A-K (2013) Visible and invisible informalities and institutional transformation. Lessons from transition countries: Georgia, Romania, Uzbekistan. In: Hayoz N, Giordano C (eds) Informality and post- socialist transition. Peter Lang, Frankfurt

Verdery K (1991) National ideology under socialism: identity and cultural politics in Ceausescu's Romania. University of California Press, Berkeley

Zarecka II (1994) Frames of remembrance: the dynamics of collective memory. Transaction Publishers, London

Chapter 8
Narratives, Networks and Policies (Sulina and Beyond)

Abstract In this chapter, we stay with Sulina but bring together the lines of inquiry on narrative and on networks. More broadly, we investigate the limits but also forms of agency of networks, physical landscapes, and other agents of the Real in narrative construction and reconstruction. We discuss the links between past, present and future that are affected by these influences, relevant when considering issues of policy and planning. The links between remembering, envisioning futures, and ongoing coordination of collective decision-making are very visible in local cosmopolitanism, and they differ according to the relation between narratives and networks.

Keywords Narrative · Network · Agency · Real · Policy · Future · Social memory · Landscape · Identity

8.1 Changing Landscapes and Reconstruction of Identity

We would like to reflect here on the relations between narratives and networks in the evolution of local cosmopolitanism in Sulina, and introduce the policy dimension more explicitly. Policies we see as coordination mechanisms of power-knowledge, as institutions coordinating actors marked by positions of power and by understandings of the world (Van Assche et al. 2011a). Policies can be formal and informal, and will transform all the time, in encounters with other actors and policies, with other actor-knowledge configurations (Van Assche et al. 2012, 2013). Planning we understand as spatial planning, as the coordination of policies and practices affecting spatial organization. Development we understand as the articulation of visions for the future of the community and acting on these visions. Governance, finally, we see as the taking of collectively binding decisions in and for the community, by a combination of governmental and non-governmental actors (Van Assche et al. 2014a). There is always governance beyond government, and there are always informal institutions beyond policies and plans (Van Assche et al. 2014b).

Moving forward in and with a community does not imply a belief in absolute progress, nor in one particular model of democracy or polity. It does assume the possibility to envision a future and use policy tools to move in that direction. It assumes that nothing is entirely stuck in the past or the present, that collective action can make a difference (Van Assche and Hornidge 2015). At the same time, the ideas about moving forwards in a community are connected to ideas about past and present, to stories about self, place and history, and to practical histories of coordination, of power relations. Visions for the future are never reducible to stories and practices of the past, but there are linkages and there are dependencies in the evolution of governance.

In governance, what can enable a way forward, and what can create obstacles, are, we believe, narratives and networks. More broadly, we can say that the discursive constructions of past, present, place and self are constrained by the Real, by networks, physical landscapes, emotional landscapes, which are resistance to free invention in the discursive world, but at the same time produce new discursivities which are not identical to the Real (Zizek 2008; Fuchs 2001). Each occurrence of the Real as resistance can lead to new discursive production, which brings a reinterpretation of the Real, a manifestation in the Symbolic and the Imaginary which disrupts and produces, unhinges and settles.

For the understanding of local cosmopolitanism, we believe that *the Real is first of all the Real of governance*, and that the productive tensions producing our realities are first of all the tensions between narratives and networks. Within governance, stories about place, self and history inspire the actions of actors, inspire the kind of policies put in place, the understandings of problems and solutions, and of more and less desirable, more and less realistic futures. The networks which are relevant are the networks of governance itself, the configurations of actors and institutions and of power and knowledge (Van Assche et al. 2012, 2014a). When analyzing local cosmopolitanism, we have to broaden both narratives and networks. The stories about self are stories about a larger world, of which this place is a special representative, the networks are also networks with other places, with other cosmopolitan places, or with a network of other places which allows for an idea of representation of the world at large (Van Assche 2014a, b).

Through the networks and narratives of governance, other manifestations of the Real affect governance. Boundaries of concepts, places and groups are discursive products, but can veil entwinings of Symbolic, Imaginary and Real (cf Jacobs and Van Assche 2014). Physical landscapes offer resistance and embody agency. Objects and architecture can have agency, physical infrastructures, presences which can alter the reproduction of networks, the production of narratives, the course of collective decision-making. Local cosmopolitanism represents not only a narrative but also an ambition, an ambition imposing special requirements on narratives and networks. While many versions of local cosmopolitanism are possible, many ideas on privileged access or better mirroring of a larger whole, present or virtual, they will have to be persuasive internally and, in the long run, externally, to survive among alternative understandings of reality (Luhmann 1995).

8.1 Changing Landscapes and Reconstruction of Identity

For Sulina, we need to mention again the forgetting of old networks, the deep forgetting of previous paragraphs, as a problem of connectivity with the Real, as a lack of understanding of real positive conditions and a lack of understanding why the past cannot be brought back and certain development visions (e.g. Palm Beach visions) do not make a lot of sense (Van Assche et al. 2009). But that is not all. We need to pay attention to the real power relations coming with the presence of purely symbolic, i.e. purely arbitrary international borders, and, in the past, with the institutional exception of the CED, an international presence at the local level, opening up new practical and narrative options. We need to mention again the nature of the physical landscape, the forces continuously remolding it.

As Barbara Hurd, in *Stirring the mud*, eloquently explored, marshes and wetland do exert a special attraction to the human imagination (Hurd 2003). Border and boundaries are blurred, between land and water, above and below, and access is difficult. This invites dreaming, blurring of perspectives and identities, and it invites straightening, reclamation, turning the landscape into something more recognizable, understandable, homey and productive, all at the same time. The Danube Delta, as a vast marshland, invited both. People fled there, to forget and be forgotten, and others, more powerful, tried to reclaim the land and control the inhabitants, to turn them into something more settled and recognizable for the powers that be (Teampău and Van Assche 2007, 2009a, b). We can see the Delta as a blank slate, a landscape of marshes and streams, fading so fast, changing in nature so irrepressibly, of people hiding and moving, a landscape thus inviting the projection of new images all the time, inviting an interpretation as empty, as a natural place, as an unsettled place, an undeveloped place. Previous presences, previous cultural complexity, was easily forgotten. In this blank swamp, Sulina was established.

The Real of the landscape constitutes agency of the landscape, but this does not mean that the actual landscape was not altered all the time (Jacobs and Van Assche 2014). It does not mean that it could escape reconfigurations of economic, political and cultural networks (Fuchs 2001). An interpretation as blank slate can lead to various projections, of triggering new policies that can have real effects. We know that in the CED era, Sulina was the focus of attention for development projects. Sulina was literally carved out of the swamps, using both natural dunes and river levies as starting point, while access to the hinterland became possible because of the jetties and dredging in the Sulina mouth and the straightening of the Sulina branch. It was only with Romanian communism that the emphasis of development moved from Sulina to the Delta, that attempts were undertaken to map out the Delta and bring it into the fold of the state. We already mentioned the scaling up and industrialization of reed production, the moving of people, land reclamation projects. A silica mine was started, with little success (Teampău 2010, 2011).

In the communist period, the emphasis was on fishing and fish processing, with additional industries associated with the never ending attempts to make the rest of the delta more 'useful' and to bring it under more direct control. Romanian and foreign expertise was mobilized to develop the delta, and the Dutch delta was one of the guiding models for Ceaușescu. Dutch government experts were flown in, to assess soil conditions and land reclamation projects (Iordachi and Van Assche 2014). Their negative assessment was not publicized and did not have consequences in Romania, since the project had to be successful. The resistance of nature to the projects, and the failure of most reclamation work was kept silent, and did not have many narrative consequences. Drainage projects were technically tough and very expensive, while in the dry uplands irrigation was similarly wasteful. Even with imposed silence and secrecy, this slowed down things, and the Complex plan for the development of the delta, was de facto a series of plans which all tripped over the Real.

Most people felt the process of "agriculturalization" as an intrusion on the part of communists. One older informant recalls: "When we went to the seaside, we would pass along the bridges, and could see the fish in the clear water, with water lilies and willows. That was very nice. But then *they* drained it. They drained it for agricultural reasons, which wasn't really productive anyway. Then they had to build the dike to protect the city from flooding, because the channels were closed. This dike compromised the beauty of the swamp. They were supposed to turn the lands into agricultural ones, but they never did it. But they destroyed the swamp in the process". People are also upset about closing the natural channels (one of them, the local photographer, is documenting local change for forty years now). Symbolically, turning these agricultural plots back to nature is also getting old Sulina back (pre-communism) (Van Assche et al. 2008: 123). Another narrative describes and emphasizes the beauty of the place before communism: "we had the canal in front of the house and used to wash and rinse cloths in the water; it was so crystal-clear, you could see the fish. The canal was communicating with Danube, and fishermen came home each day rowing their boats to the gate of the house. Now it's drowned. When going to the beach, there was a canal and was full of water lilies, you could go in and pick lots of them. It was such a beauty, such a beauty. Agriculture? It went well for a while, in the first year we had huge potatoes, but in the second year they were already pierced by the reed that was growing back. And then there was nothing, and agriculture was over" (Teampău 2013: 134).

Full reclamation was never achieved, and full control was never achieved. Still, these policies, result of and resulting in different network configurations, had impacts in many ways. They did alter the delta, its landscape, its pattern of habitation and land use, its patterns of legality and illegality, to a large extent. Since the results of development policies could not be questioned, they could not be evaluated properly, neither by locals, nor by civil servants or experts in administration. Economic benefits were minimal. Fish polders were much too large to be efficient. Reed production faltered because of machines damaging the roots. New land turned acidic quickly when exposed to air. The quality of the ecosystems was severely affected, but the mere vastness of the marshlands, the still very rich birdlife, and the still sizable fish catch veiled the ecological damage (Bell et al. 2001). That the fish caught now were not the fish caught a generation ago were not the fish caught in the 19th century, is not often observed. Changing connectivity in the ecosystem, changing water management, water quality, introduction of new fish species changing the underwater landscape, further affecting conditions for older species, all this remained obscure for most, including the European green actors who were eying the place as the last untouched European wetland when communism collapsed (Van Assche et al. 2011a, b).

According to another narrative, "the communists considered the Delta an asset and, at the beginning, they planned to turn it in a big fishery. All private fisheries were nationalized, and people need special authorization to fish. They were all turned into state registered fishermen. The vast majority of the fishermen were Lipovans and, because they were state employees, they had a privileged position like access to food rations. However, back then the situation was very different, fish was abundant and people could survive even though they had to take most of the catch to the state owned fishery" (Teampău and Van Assche 2009a: 54).

During communism, Sulina was a problem. The Delta was a technical obstacle, but also a challenge, an opportunity. There were always reports of untapped resources, despite various failed plans. The economic optimism regarding resource development dated back to the pre-communist years of Grigori Antipa, biologist, writer, promotor of conservation and development of the Delta (Iordachi and Van Assche 2014). Sulina however was different, since not a perceived emptiness inviting development but a strong presence of something not desired, a presence in physical terms and in narrative. Sulina itself shrunk considerably since the 1930s. The surviving minorities were a problem, their memories of the CED Sulina, of a larger world, of alternative development paths, of differently networked economies and social boundaries. And the memories of others, the stories elsewhere about a past which did look better than the present (Teampău and Van Assche 2009a, b).

Industrialization was understood as an objectively better way forward, since communism was supposed to rely on proletarians, people working in industries. Given the nature of the place, industrialization was first of all fish canning, and the fish came from intensified sea fishing and aquaculture on land, in a hybrid (natural/engineered) and oversized form which, as said, did not work very well. The intensification of fish production was needed for the scaling up of canneries and the creation of a communist working class culture. The demolition of bourgeois architecture on the waterfront, the building of apartments in modernist style, with communal living arrangements, was part of the same strategy. Yet the resistance of the Real which halted many development plans of the Delta also asserted itself here; plans to demolish the whole waterfront were not implemented, new apartments did not materialize, since resources were lacking, the distance too great, profits too small.

Under communism, any version of cosmopolitanism was a problem and a risk, and cherishing it in Sulina was a silent sign of resistance, of sticking to identities that were not supposed to exist or not supposed to be relevant (Teampău 2011, 2013). Keeping stories of past glories alive in the tin factory was difficult, and it was difficult in the new apartment blocks that were, with much effort, built on the water front and in the blocks further away from the water. Some significant historical buildings were destroyed, many others were not maintained, and left to private initiative for maintenance. The Greek, Armenian and Jewish houses of the nicer neighborhoods close the water were taken over by Romanian and Russian speaking groups, who used the places differently, changed the internal structure in many cases. Communal living arrangements there were not directly requested by the communists, but came with overcrowding, slow building campaigns, lack of resources for private parties to restore, renovate, or build anew (Verdery 1991). Only modest new buildings further away from the waterfront were possible and allowed as private initiative.

The urban scenery of the city, however, undergoes drastic changes. Following the war, many of the old houses were demolished, while the official propaganda presented this process as a 'renewal' of the city. Some people remember that after the war, "it was mostly empty plots and a few houses here and there, due to heavy bombing," while others remember "a stupid, unschooled mayor who, after the war was over, gave permission to destroy a lot of good, stone-made houses." According to a similar narrative, "the first thing they demolished was the Anglican church, this way all connections with the imperialists would disappear". In fact, under the apparent rebuilding of the city, many of the symbolic reminders of Sulina's "imperialist" past were intentionally destroyed and the architecture of the city transformed according to the new times (less bourgeois houses, more communist blocks of flats) (cf. Teampău and Van Assche 2009a: 52–53; Van Assche and Teampău 2009).

In Sulina, nostalgia for the former landscape of the city (illustrated by a shared remembering of the many channels that cut the place across) speaks actually about (longing for) a status quo ante. "Sulina also had a lot of river channels, made by the Commission. These had a role of communication (people would use it as a travel route) and they relieved the pressure from the Danube at high tide. When we went to the seaside, we would pass along the bridges, and could see the fish in the clear water, with water lilies and willows. That was very nice. But then they drained it. They drained it for agricultural reasons, which wasn't really productive anyway. Then they had to build the dike to protect the city from flooding, because the channels were closed. This dike compromised the beauty of the swamp" (Mrs. N.) (cf. Teampău and Van Assche 2009a: 53–54). Most inhabitants of Sulina resent the way the communist urban planning bluntly changed the local landscape (closing the natural channels and trying to transform the plots around the city for agricultural use) as a forced intrusion onto "their" city. Conversely, turning these useless agricultural plots back to nature signifies symbolically getting old Sulina back.

For a brief period, the years before Ceaucescu, the Russian speaking groups became prominent, and a past shared with neighboring Ukraine was emphasized, as well as older regional trade connections, but the position of these people, and their narrative of the place, was soon marginalized again. Whereas the war years are locally remembered as utterly destabilizing, flaming distrust, ripping apart communities, the post-war years are remembered as very poor, and associated with bully-style local government dominated by Lipovans. Stalin was next door. Ceaușescu turned away from the USSR, and very quickly, the Lipovans lost ground in local politics too (Teampău 2011). Yet, they stayed, built, welcomed newcomers from the swamps, slowly transformed the urban landscape, from the

8.1 Changing Landscapes and Reconstruction of Identity

margins, and from the seams, as water permeated Sulina from different sides, creating internal margins or seams. Of all the groups, they identified most with the place, despite its alien story. They were most motivated not to leave, despite their marginal position. They did not see many alternatives, and they made the city different, less urban, while slowly absorbing the cosmopolitan narratives. This was not a rural strategy, rather a continuation of tradition and a survival strategy under still difficult conditions, relying on skills, materials and forms of organization they were familiar with. Whenever communism was weaker locally, did not impose collective work of some sort, or offer work of any sort, fishing and fishing in teams was always a way to survive (Bell et al. 2001; cf Iordachi and Dobrincu 2009). The Lipovans were in this sense closest to the landscape, and the vagaries of power, the ever changing presence and grip of ideology (Verdery 1991; Smith 1998), left spaces where the Real of the landscape asserted itself and allowed spaces for the Lipovans, more easily than for others.

Of course, the landscape is not the only Real in human societies, and the communist regime might have had a checkered record locally, it did leave a legacy locally of new power structures, with networks (including some Lipovan elements) of local families at least able to work with the communists still occupying positions of power. Locals who knew how to promise, to show something expected, to accept that promises from the other side could be broken, who knew the resource flows (in factories, fish farms, shops, professional associations,…) could occupy places to tap these flows, which helped them to remain in place (Teampău and Van Assche 2007). Another communist legacy is that these networks are highly opaque, because they were not supposed to exist, and because, also then, there was a mutual distrust between the higher level administrations and local government (cf Iordachi and Dobrincu 2009). For locals and outsiders alike, Sulina and the Delta were clearly not model communist places, because of the marginal location, marginal development and because of their suspicious histories. A history of linkage with the larger world was an obstruction now for becoming a model communist place. The narratives of old networks made new networks less likely (cf Fuchs 2001; Luhmann 1995). It looks like there were attempts under communism to appoint outsiders to rule locally, and to spearhead the development efforts by the regional development company based in Tulcea (employing several thousands in the 1970s). From what we could gather, it also looks like the local networks, partly in and partly outside the party organs, were never broken, during and after Ceaușescu.

A comprehensive, very detailed reconstruction of the linkages between shifting networks, changing landscapes, and the narrative dynamics in Sulina and the delta is not possible within the limitations of this short treatise. We do believe to have illustrated here the tensions, sometimes productive, sometimes less, between networks and narratives in Sulina. Local cosmopolitanism as narrative is easier to maintain than as network, and also other manifestations of the Real can thwart attempts to maintain it as lived reality. Local cosmopolitanism has to be understood as input and output of local governance, as strategic tool and as narrative source of identification and grounding. When it is seen as negative, it can still have productive effects, e.g. through inspiring resistance, and keeping identities and place narratives alive. While the Real undermined alternative development paths, and while the Real underpinnings of the CED Sulina were largely forgotten, there was a memory of local cosmopolitanism as something that had been real. This lent a credibility to it which made it more potent in keeping resistance alive and made the past look more realistic than the present. The present was perceived to lead nowhere, and was not real since all promises were broken, and real information was scarce and dangerous when possessed. The idea of living a lie sheds a different light on the past. In this case, a cosmopolitan past offered inspiration for an alternative path.

It is hard to map out completely the implications of changing networks and obdurate landscapes for the narrative construction and reconstruction of cosmopolitanism in Sulina, and the functions of those narratives in daily lives. Yet the mechanisms can be observed, and their relevance for evolving governance demonstrated. In the next section, we come back to the place of the tensions between narrative in network in governance. We pay attention again to the reconstructions of the past in evolving governance, in the making and evading of policies, in the construction of collective futures, and we pay attention to local cosmopolitanism in this dynamics.

8.2 Past, Future and Policy

Policies affect realities and hit the wall of realities (Zizek 2008; Luhmann 1995). Cosmopolitan narratives enable cosmopolitan realities and hit the wall of others. Sulina had a memory of centrality and marginality, surrounded by an area with a long history of mostly marginality. The centrality of Sulina was a grand exception, also highlighted by the landscape differences. Local cosmopolitanism was more special because of the contrast, more valuable, and sometimes more dangerous.

For Sulina, we would argue, the history of marginality is more important than the history of centrality, than the CED era, and its local cosmopolitanism. We illustrated the importance of older histories of exploitation and marginalization, and of more recent histories of environmental governance (the delta being managed as a natural area since 1991). That same history of marginality has implications for, currently promoted, participatory multi-level governance too, in which participation in various arena's is required. Locals are not always ready, are imbued with versions of the past which inspire impossible futures.

We argue that a better understanding of the balance between narrative and network in local cosmopolitanism can avoid tripping over the Real, can avoid the pursuit of futures which are not likely to materialize, and the reliance on policy instruments which are unlikely to work. In the case of Sulina, the unwanted effects of a history of marginality show themselves in the lack of insight in what made it all possible, and the lack of insight in the need for present coordination at the local level and coordination with other levels of governance (Van Assche et al. 2009). The selection of forgetting and remembering that came out of the tough history of

8.2 Past, Future and Policy

the place, enabled the survival of a local cosmopolitanism, as a counter-discourse against green futures, as a former counter-discourse against Romanian communist nationalism. The vision of the cosmopolitan past didn't fit entirely with the experience of the present, but the place now still allowed for an interpretation as cosmopolitan in essence, as a virtual reality which could spark the same effects again in the future. Old differences can be reinterpreted more directly in the mold of a revived multi-culturalism and cosmopolitanism. The local version of cosmopolitanism relies on the past, and on the survival of buildings, and traces of old ethnic and cultural distinctions, acquiring new significance.

Despite the small size of the town, of the population, despite the rarity of infrastructures on which to revive cosmopolitanism, the uses and versions of local cosmopolitanism are varied. In some cases, they serve as facade for short term gains, or for pushing development that would have been sold under different stories otherwise (Van Assche et al. 2012). In other cases, it inspires visions of a new free port, of a new cosmopolitan cachet. Another discourse, influenced by different traveling concepts and hegemonic discourses, is a version of the future as spring break paradise, as Palm Beach Florida. Connectivity, the restoration of a lost connectivity, is a key word in that discourse, and it can be linked to the other futures conjured up and inspired by local cosmopolitanism. Strategy and identity cannot always be separated, and a cosmopolitan argument in a commercial or political discussion can be linked to a real belief in this identity of place, and a belief that revival of old glories is possible (Van Assche et al. 2014a; Beunen et al. 2015).

For other actors, at regional and national level, the green future of the Delta is more obvious, although, for some, it is clear that the current Reserve designation is not enough to actually preserve anything. Critics of local/regional governance are usually pleading for more effective nature conservation. Some, such as the World Bank in the 1990s, and the European Bank for Reconstruction and Development, were convinced that a form of sustainable development, supported by more participatory governance, was the way forward. They withdrew their support (EBRD) or criticized their own projects (WB) because it did not appear to them that the conditions were ready for participatory development (Van Assche et al. 2011a, b). It looked to them that local and regional networks undermined more inclusive development strategies and effective nature conservation. Even those who promoted more participatory development, did not envision a cultural complexity in the past, and certainly not a cosmopolitan past and hoped for future for Sulina. They tended to start from the blank slate idea, the swamp where for some reason some people ended up.

The green actors which focused entirely on nature conservation, such as the Biosphere Administration in its early days, and several nature organizations, seemed to start entirely from the idea of a blank slate, unfortunately touched by the communists, and, alas, inhabitants. In that perspective, Sulina was absent or excluded from the Delta, local in general were treated as either lost in the swamp, or criminalized. Fishing, the traditional livelihood of most of them, and for many a survival skill, after other job opportunities disappeared, was perceived as damaging nature, and the locals as main enemy of the Biosphere Reserve. The contrast with the dreams and hopes in Sulina could not have been bigger. Whereas the initial militaristic approach to nature conservation faded out after international complaints, the position of people in the Danube Delta is still not clear for many actors, and a version of sustainable development which includes a different Sulina did not emerge yet (Van Assche et al. 2011a, 2012, 2013). The zones in the Delta where economic use is permitted are mostly zones for the well connected concessionaires, not zones where a combination of uses resulted from inclusive governance. For many in the Delta, an experience of exclusion by the Biosphere Administration, at a time when finally communism had disappeared, created new images of nature and the Delta, mostly negative, while it revived images of the old cosmopolitan Sulina. Sometimes, nature and cosmopolitanism were opposed, and deemed impossible to combine in future policies, whereas in other, rarer, entrepreneurial, cases, there was an understanding of a possible commodification of both, a restoration of both nature and culture which could benefit everyone.

Combinations of environmental design and heritage design as an appropriate future for Sulina and its surrounding (cf Van Assche and Hornidge 2015; Arendt 1999), inspired by its cosmopolitan past (relegated to the past) and its green past and present, are rarely found locally, except with people in direct contact with the administrative and academic networks that have formed around the new and green Delta. For us, authors, such future seems an appropriate path which could bridge many difference, which could provide a basis for sustainable development. Yet such strategy can only be sustainable when locally supported. That does not mean that it has to be entirely a bottom-up strategy, that everyone needs to be on board, or that governance has to be entirely based on participation. It does mean, we believe, that locals need to be convinced that it makes sense, maybe not initially, but after a while, when results become visible. If however deep forgetting created a local cosmopolitanism which inspires utterly unrealistic futures, and there are few to politely contradict, if nature is a deeply traumatized construct because of marginalization old and new, and if participatory governance is distrusted and associated with fake participation organized by regional actors under pressure, the conditions for establishing such procedural and substantive frame are not fertile.

If we look back at our stories of Sulina and the Danube Delta, we can discern a few recurring issues. Constructions of the past influence the articulation of visions for the future, in substance, but also in the way things are organized. Remembering and forgetting affects the visions of the future which are possible, and the forms of coordination which can be imagined and trusted. In governance, trust is performative; it creates realities by changing modes of participation (Van Assche et al. 2012, 2014a). Contact with the world at large, seeing what works elsewhere, and understanding what worked in the past, helps to figure out what can work in the future, how the community can find agreement, can be mobilized, can mobilize others, to define a future. A history of marginality and deep forgetting creates obstacles for moving forwards. Local cosmopolitanism survived in Sulina, because it acquired ever changing rhetorical and political values, but its framing power for desirable futures is limited and problematic, because of the particular position and history of Sulina.

Local cosmopolitanism in Sulina came to rely more and more on narrative, and on a more and more impoverished narrative, less on an understanding of the Real past and present, of old networks, natural conditions, power relations. The Symbolic and the Imaginary, both powerful sources of policy, led to discourses of past and present which were able to ignore aspects of the Real because of the relative isolation for a long time, in a community which fantasized without being confronted with the actual needs of coordination, policy making, investment, and without being confronted with the darker sides and the more practical sides of the CED past.

Which means we have to come back to the topic of shifting networks, and investigate the impact of these shifts on the relation between social memory, narrating the past and the place in the past, and on the other hand constructions of the future and the desirable future. For local cosmopolitanism to offer avenues to new futures, we would say that an understanding in governance of the tensions between networks and narratives, an understanding of the disruptive forces of the Real is essential. This is true when old positions of centrality are lost, and it is true when there is more left of a cosmopolitan character. Conjuring up images of a past to be regained, or a centrality to be extended into time and space, can be productive in policy; it can be a strategy of productive mystification, be performative. But it can, as we know by now, trip over the Real.

Understanding the versions, history, and functions of cosmopolitanism will help. Reflexivity will be helpful, in governance and in the community more broadly. Indeed, cosmopolitanism is always local, is always tinged by local histories and identifications and networks as visible and transformed in governance, and this makes each local cosmopolitanism different. The image of self, of the world, of a privileged relation, and of the reason of privilege, ought to be investigated not once but interrogated over and over again in governance. Without this, the Real will irrepressibly assert itself, and fantasies of centrality will become fantasies with less and less effect and with less and less auspicious influence on policy-making.

References

Arendt R (1999) Growing greener. Island Press, Washington

Bell S, Nichersu I, Ionescu L, Iacovici E (2001) Conservation versus livelihood in the Danube Delta. Anthropol East Eur Rev 19(1):11–15

Beunen R, Van Assche K, Duineveld M (2015) Evolutionary governance theory: theory and applications. Springer, Heidelberg

Fuchs S (2001) Against essentialism. Harvard University Press, Cambridge

Hurd B (2003) Stirring the mud: on swamps, bogs, and human imagination. Houghton Mifflin Harcourt, New York

Iordachi C, Dobrincu D (eds) (2009) Transforming peasants, property and power: the collectivization of agriculture in Romania, 1949–1962. Central European University Press, Hungary

Iordachi C, Van Assche K (2014) The bio-politics of the Danube Delta. Lexington/Rowman & Littlefield, New York

Jacobs J, Van Assche K (2014) Understanding empirical boundaries: a systems-theoretical avenue in border studies. Geopolitics 19(1):182–205
Luhmann N (1995) Social systems. Stanford University Press, Stanford
Smith G (ed) (1998) Nation-building in the post-Soviet borderlands: the politics of national identities. Cambridge University Press, Cambridge
Teampău P (2010) Sulina traita de Panait Zachis. EFES, Cluj
Teampău P (2011) Sulina, alta lume, alta viata. EFES, Cluj
Teampău P (2013) Sulina fabuloasa. EFES, Cluj
Teampău P, Van Assche K (2007) Sulina, the dying city in a vital region: social memory and nostalgia for the European future. Ethnologia Balkanica 11(1):257–278
Teampău P, Van Assche K (2009a) Migratory marginalities: making sense of home, self and mobility. Ethnologia Balkanica 13:147–163
Teampău P, Van Assche K (2009b) 'Sulina, Sulina, when there's water, there's no light: memory and autobiography in a Romanian town', identities. J Polit Gend Cult 7(1–2):33–70
Van Assche K (2014a) Ernest oberholtzer and the art of boundary crossing: writing, life and the narratives of conservation and planning. Plan Perspect 29(1):45–65
Van Assche K (2014b) Semiotics of silent lakes: Sigurd Olson and the interlacing of writing, policy and planning. J Environ Policy Plan (ahead-of-print) 1–15
Van Assche K, Hornidge AK (2015) Rural development: knowledge and expertise in governance. Wageningen Academic, Wageningen
Van Assche K, Teampău P (2009) Layered encounters: urban palimpsest and the performance of multiculturalism in the Romanian Danube Delta. Anthropol East Eur Rev 27(1):7–19
Van Assche K, Teampău P, Devlieger P, Suciu C (2008) Liquid boundaries in marginal marshes. Reconstructions of identity in the Romanian Danube Delta. Studia Sociologia 53(1):15–133
Van Assche K, Devlieger P, Teampău P, Verschraegen G (2009) Remembering and forgetting in the margin: constructing past and future in the Romanian Danube Delta. Memory Studies 2(2):211–234
Van Assche K, Duineveld M, Beunen R, Teampău P (2011a) Delineating locals: transformations of knowledge/power and the governance of the Danube Delta. J Environ Policy Plan 13(1):1–21
Van Assche K, Beunen R, Jacobs J, Teampău P (2011b) Crossing trails in the marshes: flexibility and rigidity in the governance of the Danube Delta. J Environ Plan Manage 54(8):997–1018
Van Assche K, Bell S, Teampău P (2012) Traumatic natures in the swamp: concepts of nature and participatory governance in the Danube Delta. Environ Values 21(2):163–183
Van Assche K, Shtaltovna A, Hornidge A-K (2013) Visible and invisible informalities and institutional transformation: lessons from transition countries: Georgia, Romania, Uzbekistan. In: Hayoz N, Giordano C (eds) Informality and post-socialist transition. Peter Lang, Frankfurt
Van Assche K, Beunen R, Duineveld M (2014a) Evolutionary governance theory: an introduction. Springer, Heidelberg
Van Assche K, Beunen R, Duineveld M (2014b) Formal/informal dialectics and the self-transformation of spatial planning systems: an exploration. Adm Soc 46(6):654–683
Verdery K (1991) National ideology under socialism: identity and cultural politics in Ceausescu's Romania. University of California Press, Berkeley
Zizek S (2008) In defense of lost causes. Verso, London

Part IV
Small and Large

Chapter 9
Local Cosmopolitanism and Governance

Abstract In this chapter, we bring back the comparison with Trieste, Odessa and Tbilisi, confront this with our initial theoretical frame, and take stock of its development. We discuss the image of local cosmopolitanism and its local construction we obtained after our investigations, and what this image means for a general perspective on globalization. Zooming in, we then return to the question of policy relevance: what can our analysis tell us about the implications of cosmopolitanism for policy, how and why should policy and planning envision a cosmopolitan future or past, what are the possibilities and limits of steering in this.

Keywords Local cosmopolitanism · Globalization · Policy · Steering · Real · Žižek · Governance · Trieste · Odessa · Tbilisi

9.1 Introduction: Local Cosmopolitanism Revisited

What is local cosmopolitanism? Let us take another look at Trieste, Tbilisi, Odessa and Sulina. All our places are cities with a cosmopolitan past cherished in the present. Sulina is unique, in terms of narrative dynamics and network dynamics. But also what we observed there can be found elsewhere, the mechanisms pertaining to memory, to the blurring of past and present, part and whole. We still need a deeper reflection on the relation between narratives and networks. We know that local cosmopolitanism, in its emergence and maintenance, in its basking in privilege, relies on both, on a particular tension between both. When does a place, a community gives rise to local cosmopolitanism? One can easily refer to connections, to diversity internal, to diversity in connections, to larger conceptual frames which enable dealing with and understanding the world, to ideas of superiority, either preceding or coming after the other forms of connectivity and representativeness.

These can represent different versions of cosmopolitanism. They are all local in the sense that what can be told, what can be persuasive, and what can be done, results from local evolutions, from local interpretations of larger narratives, of local adaptations to larger networks, of understandings of the world that are always localized when they are acted upon. We speak explicitly about cosmopolitan places, not individuals, and we do not refer to the enlightenment ideals of cosmopolitan justice and equality. For us, the substance of cosmopolitanism is nothing, emptiness (cf Žižek 2000). Cosmopolitanism simply means a privileged access, a closer relation between the part and the whole. But the part can only act on an image of the whole which is produced according to conditions pertaining to the part. The world we act upon, also if we believe ourselves privileged, is a world we construct. If we act in a coordinated manner, as a community governing itself, then we deal with a variety of narratives of the whole which can coexist at a time and place but can also merge and will in governance and coexistence likely adapt to each other (Van Assche et al. 2014a, b; Latour 2009). Logician Spencer-Brown speaks of a re-entry, the return of the whole in the part, as an image, framed by the part (Luhmann 1995). Communities and governance networks in communities can produce their own perspectives, their own understandings of themselves and the world. There is no overarching perspective which sees the world 'as it is' and which grasps the relation between parts and whole in an objective manner (Luhmann 1990; Van Assche et al. 2014a, b; Beunen et al. 2015; Miller 2002). There are global phenomena, but their effects and their understanding will vary per place and according to the perspective taken. The responses to these phenomena rely on internal complexity of communities and the understanding of the world this produces (Delanty 2009).

In Peircean terms, the part can refer to the whole in iconic, symbolical and indexical manners (Van Assche 2004; van Zoest 1978). The reference can be actual and potential, real or virtual (Shields 2013). An iconic reference to the whole can entail a visual form of cosmopolitanism, relying on visual signs, on architecture, dress, urban design. It relies on a unity which has to exist, but does not have to be there. An indexical reference relies on contiguity, as explained earlier. It relies on a presence now, not just existence. One can imagine an indexical cosmopolitanism as driven by the Real, by existing networks producing effects of resemblance, of special access (Latour 2009; Žižek 2008). One can imagine symbolic cosmopolitanism as relying on symbolic references, references that could have been different, result of convention. Symbolic cosmopolitanism is a matter of stories, stories which do not have to imply any truth, any real connection with a larger whole which is as it is said to be.

Actual cosmopolitanism is then what somehow links in a particular way to the world at large, through networks and narratives, in a manner where the Real, the Symbolic and the Imaginary are entwined, as in what otherwise be could reality. Virtual cosmopolitanism is what is told, what is present in narrative, narrative of the past and the present, but which could become real, which could become performative, lead to actions, to policies which might re-network the community. The past can never come back, and a return to it is always imagined, yet the attempt to restore lost networks and a lost form of cosmopolitanism can create a new one in a world that is always re-networked, transformed, and a community which never allows for the same entry to the larger world. The virtual thus holds a promise;

9.1 Introduction: Local Cosmopolitanism Revisited

it is a potential cosmopolitanism, more than simply an imagined one. Stories have power, as discourse, and certainly discourse leading to policies, to coordinated action and plans for action, can be performative (Miller 2002; Van Assche et al. 2014a, b; Yanow 2000). The discourse has to be persuasive, convince others inside and outside the community that there is a possibility that this might become true, that cooperation can work, that others can be trusted to work in that direction (Gunder 2003; Van Assche et al. 2009). The discursive configurations in and around the community make certain discursive coalitions more likely than others, and certain forms of collective action. If discursive coalitions are formed, the networks of the various actors can be mutually beneficial and can act as one networks, where new transformations of knowledge/power can take place (Easterly 2014).

Which brings us once more to the relation between network and narrative dynamics in determining the forms and functions of local cosmopolitanism. Knowledge/power transformations take place in networks, but also alter networks (Latour 2009; Van Assche and Hornidge 2015).

For the sake of simplicity, we previously equated networks with the Real, with an aspect of reality which sometimes defies symbolization and disrupts imagination. For our analysis of cosmopolitanism, this holds mostly true. The realities of networks do erode and simply halt fantasies of cosmopolitanism past and present. However, new understandings arise when we, with Žižek, locate, in a transmutation of Marxist insight, the Real in both networks and narratives (Žižek 2008, 2013). Narratives can drive networks and narratives can drive network change, while economic or political networks are simultaneously marked by their internal logics, by the capability of internal changes sparking off changes elsewhere in the network (Hajer and Wagenaar 2003; Fischer 2000, 2009; Roe 1994). Networks, in other words, offer resistance to stories, but cannot exist without stories (Fuchs 2001). They limit the performative effects of stories, but some performative effects are best described as network change. What is easier, still, is create narratives. What is less easy, is to find an audience which is willing to believe, to cooperate, to reshuffle internal networks, analyze external networks, and figure out a strategy to navigate and possibly transform them. Constant evaluation is recommended: which networking, which narrative, which fit, which form of cosmopolitanism can we realistically envision and sell (Miller and Fox 2007)?

9.2 The Real

In Žižek's view, a view trying to stay true to Marxist tenets, the economic domain remains the Real, as that which is driving the essential changes in societies, as that which is disturbing and limiting policies and polities (exemplified by Žižek 2008, but present in much of his later work). For Žižek, capitalism won, and did so by incorporating its own resistance as source of innovation, similar to Foucault's statements about power including its own resistance, as shaking up the terrain to reveal where and what kind of resistance exists, in order to orient itself, to learn, to recuperate. Neo-liberalism, for him and for many leftist geographers, sociologists and other academics, is then the big enemy which cannot be beaten anymore. Neo-liberalism becomes synonymous with capitalism, and an ever expanding capitalism is interpreted as that which is rendering social policies, alternative models of society, more substantive models of justice and redistribution impossible (Whatmore 2006). Neo-liberalism is also interpreted as that what makes the world more and more the same, what makes cosmopolitanism as either a matter of glossy city marketing and star architects, or a matter of showing a bit faster the next step in capitalist development, presumably because of a central position in networks of exchange and accumulation (Delanty 2009; Mignolo 2000).

While these forms of cosmopolitanism exist, we argue they are far from the only ones. While new forms of globalization can be analyzed as expanding markets, there are simultaneously new borders and boundaries which assert themselves, new identities, new flows, new relations between economic, political, legal, scientific and religious domains, in other words, different models of democracy that pop up around the world, and new forms of non-democracy. Capitalism is varied and variegated indeed, and the term capitalism suggest a unity that never existed. The Real of capitalism or neo-liberalism, is not the Real which can be observed in the transformations of places and communities. Looking at cosmopolitanism should give a clear picture of the larger forces driving change, but this offers a glimpse at places that always were hybrids between models of democracies, and always represented a specific form of self-reproduction, giving a particular form of privileged access to the world (Van Assche and Hornidge 2015; Beunen et al. 2015).

A first modification of Žižek's stance could be that economic, political and to a lesser extent artistic and scientific networks (including their use and production of expertise) as drivers of social change and producers of reality cannot easily be ignored in the narrative dynamics that can be observed more easily. Cultural capital is usually also important in different ways, cannot rely usually on its artistic understandings of the world to exert influence. Yet the spread of these ideas, the dissemination of artistic discourse which can alter the understanding of self, world and place, thus possibly triggering political and economic effects later, requires artistic networks first of all, in addition to media, to ways to economically and politically survive, to links with those networks. Thus, each domain relies on its own networks, and on linkages with the others (Fuchs 2001; cf Luhmann 1990, 1995). Another way to say this is that no functional domain in society can survive by itself. They can only exist in reference to and as complement of each other. What comes first is not always the same and not always clear. There is not always a substructure and a superstructure. And what can be described substructure, as driver, in one case, cannot be assumed to play the same elsewhere.

In romanticism, art played a different role in relation to politics than now, inspiring new identifications associated with new grand political projects, in turn reconfiguring economic landscapes. More recently, the rise of China economically cannot be simply interpreted as a victory of capitalism, since its policies are breaking all possible rules of capitalism, including the ones regarding situations where no rules are supposed to intervene. As the institutional economists demonstrated, markets exist in many shapes and forms, and are always constituted and stabilized by politics, politics which rests on narratives of place and self, and on networked forms of organization and understanding (e.g. Easterly 2014). Also in terms of human needs, and needs of communities, one cannot say unequivocally which functional domain comes first. People do not need one thing more than another, and communities do not need a capitalist form of organization more than a democratic form of politics or a common law sort of legal system. Communities in fact need very little survive as community; many equilibria and functional divisions are possible, many relations between politics, law, economy, arts and science (Luhmann 1995). The forces of economic globalization observed by many of its critics are just as much forces of politics, while in the past they could be forces of science or art, and in the future of religion (Jacobs 2014; Delanty 2009). What is first cause, or efficient cause, or final cause, or material cause in Aristotelean terms, will be different. A scientific innovation can scream for economic or political change, while elsewhere, politics can coordinate scientific innovation or lean on the research carried out by companies.

In other words, the way the world moves forward cannot be grasped so easily in terms of a universal Hegelian spirit, a zeitgeist, nor in the form of a winning neo-liberal economic substructure, nor of a legalist universalism based on human rights, and places cannot more easily participate in this forward movement by being tapped into the more relevant networks, or being able to capture a nodal position. Cosmopolitanism cannot be reduced to a more correct reflection of the current order, future order, or a more efficient access to the singular driving forces of progress. The order is diversified, is differentiated, and that growing diversity in functional systems, in operationally closed systems of narrative and discourse, as well as of networked forms of coordination, is probably the only zeitgeist we could speak of realistically, the only form of globalization, of world society, we can take seriously (cf Stichweh 2000; Teubner 1997).

Whereas cosmopolitanism was always local, that localism can now be more, rather than less, diversified. On the other hand, what it means to be cosmopolitan is not so easily grasped anymore, and the wavering discourses on it, the rapidly successive architectural, urbanist, artistic, managerial, political fashions regarding centrality, testify to this. Cities, cosmopolitan places, are supposed to be this, not that, no rather that. The creative class is supposed to make the place more cosmopolitan thus successful. Place branding is the solution. Smart growth. Lower taxes bring in the right people and companies. Parties and golf courts. Festivals. Museums. Attracting and emphasizing cultural diversity. Ethnic diversity. Ethnic entrepreneurship, tapping into unique skills and networks. High tech clusters. Universities. But then more applied, engaged. There is more place for strategy, and more tolerance for ambiguity and complexity is required. One can add: a higher degree of reflexivity in governance, regarding narratives, networks, their matching and navigation (Beunen et al. 2015; Fischer 2009). What a city 'is' and how it links and could link up to networks and narratives to craft a new form of cosmopolitanism, shows new flexibilities, but requires more dexterity in turning virtuality into reality.

Not this or that network can be considered the only hard barrier to narrative and policy aiming at a cosmopolitan position (Jacobs 2014; Jacobs and van Assche

2014; Van Assche et al. 2009). The value of past centrality will differ. Yet networks as such can be regarded a harder resistance than narrative, in the sense that their invention and construction takes more time and effort. New narratives cannot ignore networks for long, if there is an intention to make implementable policy. Meanwhile we do not reduce the Real to a substructure of networks, and, as said, acknowledge that narratives and networks continuously transform each other (Fuchs 2001; Van Assche et al. 2014a, b; Van Assche 2014a, b). We do believe that the networks have a different relation with the Real than the narrative dynamics, which are necessarily more tied to the symbolic order, and the imaginary order driving the desiring engine of identification and aspiration (Gunder 2003).

With Lacan and Žižek we would like to distinguish between the Real Real, the Imaginary Real and the Symbolic Real (Žižek 2013). The symbolic Real is the real showing itself in the symbolic order, and distinguishing it can be useful because what we can actually observe of the Real is its manifestations in the other orders. The symbolic Real is then what offers resistance to certain explanations, and we know already that this can be the reality of networks, of power, of materiality (Whatmore 2006; Jacobs and Van Assche 2014). And we know that what is behind this disturbance can still be a hybrid of symbolic, real and imaginary, as exemplified by networks which offer resistance to narrative and policy, but whose structure and function can be understood only as including narratives (cf already Pressman and Wildavsky 1984). When observing the resistance, one cannot at the same time observe where it comes from. It takes a different perspective to grasp the history of the network offering resistance, and the specific entwining of Real, Symbolic and Imaginary there (Fuchs 2001; Teubner 1997). Just as a boundary can be hard and empirical, yet hide an entwining of material and symbolic, cultural and natural elements (Jacobs and Van Assche 2014). The imaginary Real is then what punches through the attempts to orient and identify in a certain direction, because of now forgotten old identifications and orientations, in Freudian fashion (Van Assche et al. 2009; Mignolo 2000). For Lacan, for Žižek and for us, this can apply to individuals and to cultures and communities. A trauma, an inferiority complex, a relation with power, with the word, with a natural surrounding, can steer future identifications and policies in ways that are not observed in the community (Žižek 2008). The Real Real is per definition a paradox, as it is supposed to be a disruption sui generis, without a manifestation in another order. Žižek speaks of feelings of horror, experiences of emptiness, suddenly, out of nothing, not associated with difficult symbolization. Mute natures, horrifying natures and spiritual natures can reveal themselves. Silence can open the door.

9.3 Trieste and the Others

In local cosmopolitanism, the history of the community, the way it understands itself, puts it on a track to certain perceived and desired forms of relation to the world at large. The Real of networks, the Real of materiality, of power, assert themselves in

9.3 Trieste and the Others

stories losing persuasive character, in the symbolic Real, and in the lack of steering power in and by communities, the impossibility to come to policy and implement it, a lack which can be related to all three aspects of the Real as resistance.

In Trieste, a place which saw itself as the commercial center of the Habsburg Empire, what stopped working was the Empire itself. Any identification with the Empire lost persuasion after it collapsed. It lost the power to orient fantasies for a future depending on it, and it lost the role of father figure, of something one relied on while contesting it. The protection which came from the Empire stopped, yet old protection mechanism left a mark, e.g. in the urban architecture and planning which mostly took form in a period of ambiguous relations with Vienna, but which very much betrays the Habsburg mold. It left a mark on the economic life, with insurance companies being big enough to stand on their own feet and engage in international competition. The Real of new networks asserted itself when young Italy barely embraced the former commercial mastodon, and treated it as a second rate, and rather suspicious new addition. A new narrative of identification was present, of Italian unity and belonging, but this proved not very rewarding in this situation, and the older networks of Venetian cultural hegemony and Habsburg political hegemony were not acknowledged in the new narrative of Italy, including the narrative of its past. Meanwhile, in the city, the Slavic groups felt more excluded than before, and did not identify anymore with an idea of a mix representing cosmopolis. A new image of cosmopolitan Trieste had to be created through local retelling and through literature, through the works of Magris, Morris and others. After the iron curtain fell, the Habsburg Empire and its Central Europe could be rediscovered, while the European Union was ready to erode national loyalties, and this made it easier for Trieste to redefine itself as cosmopolitan, as a reminder of a larger unity now defunct but still relevant, in its traces and in its prefiguration of a European future.

Odessa, we know, has more difficulties in confronting the Real, and reinventing itself as cosmopolitan. It also moved to a different country, the USSR, and later Ukraine, and it cast itself more and more in a Russian light, with the cosmopolitan narrative relegated to the domain of folklore, and to occasions where nothing non-Russian actually has to be included in decision-making. For internal consumption, in Odessa, this might work, but even for internal Ukrainian audiences, this is not a persuasive narrative. Working with Ukrainian actors seems necessary to re-embed Odessa in the necessary networks to maintain a cosmopolitan image, and use this to envision a future of expanding networks and sustainable cosmopolitanism. The economic importance of Odessa did not decline as much as that of Trieste—it was important under the Soviets and is still the major Ukrainian port—and that helps to maintain a sense of civic pride, and a non-examination of the unraveling networks and reduced diversity. For a cosmopolitan revival of Odessa, it seems to us that the imaginary Real and the symbolic Real conspire to create obstacles. At different scales of governance, with different actors, the current identification strategy will not inspire cooperation, and the ruling interpretation of the past and present are not persuasive to attract attention and do not lead to policies which can persuasively present a path to a more central position again.

Tbilisi, meanwhile, has perhaps the least common form of cosmopolitan history, although also one which led from more to less internal complexity, from a more to a less networked position. It shares a Soviet past with Odessa, and received a lot of investment in research and development. It shares a Russian past as well. Before Russia came, however, Tbilisi functioned as the political, cultural and economic center of the Caucasus for centuries. Cosmopolitanism histories now are a card to play in a new networking towards the west. An emphasis on a rich past, an inclusive past, multi-cultural and cosmopolitan since well-connected, combines with styles of development (e.g. also on the coast) which deliberately reflect an internationalist capitalist architecture. The anticipated cosmopolitan future is a hybrid of European and American capitalism, for which the multi-cultural existence at the crossroads of Asia and Europe prepared it. Nato membership and EU membership were awaited and expected, and a general willingness to move in a more democratic, less corrupt direction, and to move fast (under Saakashvili) were understood as probably enough. Yet the West wasn't sure what to do with Georgia and when Russia took part of its territory in 2008, no Western assistance materialized. Afterwards, the feeling of moving fast into the larger world, and of being prepared, became less strong, the story less convincing. Tbilisians felt more isolated again, the crossroads idea less utilized, in a situation where clearly borders were harder than ever before. Geopolitics remains important, and the pipeline connecting the Caspian and Black Seas, offering a rare non-Russian route for Caspian and Central Asian oil, keeps Georgia on the map for international players, keeps it connected in a way not envisioned in public discourse.

Sulina is the most extreme case, most shriveled and most traumatized, subjected to the most dramatic reversal of fortunes. And, it is the case we studied most in detail, as we expected more clarity in the mechanisms of remembering and obstacles to revival for local cosmopolitanism. For Sulina, what we called deep forgetting, the loss of conditions for remembering, the forgetting of forgetting, resulting from a history of marginality, makes it extremely unlikely that the town will reclaim something akin to centrality. It also made it unlikely that policies and plans come up which understand this, which see that the future cannot be anything like the past. Opportunities to capitalize on the past, to still commodify the cosmopolitan past as an asset, elude decision-makers caught up in local network struggles and cosmopolitan fantasies (Van Assche et al. 2011a, b).

9.4 Towards a Governance Frame

The more detailed study of Sulina made it possible to confirm and extend some of the theoretical points made in the introductory chapters. We link them again in these final paragraphs, and fit them more clearly in a policy-oriented frame.

Local cosmopolitanism refers to an idea of place and community and it refers to a functioning of that community. For an understanding of the idea, we started with the analysis of narrative, for the understanding of the functioning we started

9.4 Towards a Governance Frame

from a network concept. Local governance, the taking of collectively binding decisions, is the place where functioning and ideas meet, where ideas come in and are transformed, where ideas can have impact on the functioning (Van Assche et al. 2014a, b; Beunen et al. 2015). How a place relates to the world, is understood, and altered in and through governance, through actors working together, coordinating action, articulating visions for the future, using formal and informal institutions, policies, laws and plans.

Both past and present play a role in the construction of visions for the future. Past and present are understood via ideas, via concepts, narratives, discourses. Prismatic concepts, as lenses to see the other concept, are place identity, social identity and images of history. Images of places include references to histories, while histories include references to place and to groups, while they are written from the perspective of groups and places (Van Assche 2004; Delanty 2009). The histories, places and groups present in a community, and present in governance, are thus entwined and are likely to have consequences for the understanding of the position of the place in the larger world, and of the possible futures for the community. Forgotten histories can leave traces, as can forgotten places, vanished places and people. They can leave narrative traces and they can leave traces in the actual coordination in governance, in the internal and external networks or lack thereof (Teubner 1997; Fuchs 2001; Luhmann 1990). Forgetting is thus not an innocent activity, and neither is remembering (Van Assche et al. 2009). Governance is marked by strong path dependencies, interdependence, and goal dependence, by strong legacies of the past (in narrative and in functioning), strong networked relations between actors and institutions, and by particular effects of visions for the future in a given community. The effects of plans, policies, and also legally coded ideas for a desirable future will differ per community, depending on its actor/institution configuration, power/knowledge configuration and its dependencies, which can be understood as rigidities in the governance path, as constraints on the freedom in decision-making and visioning (Latour 2009; Pressman and Wildavsky 1984; Van Assche and Hornidge 2015; Van Assche et al. 2013).

The visions for the future that come up in a governance path, and the tools to move in that direction, are products of the path: the semantics available in governance, the understandings of self, place, past and future, will structure the discussions and the visions for the future, while the history of coordination will allow for some coordinative tools and not others. The understanding of actual networks, and of actual potential for coordination internally and actual modification and re-linking externally, derives from the same semantic potential present or absent in governance (Fuchs 2001; Fischer 1990). In other words, governance needs to understand the community, the world, and first of all itself, if dreams of cosmopolitanism and especially revived cosmopolitanism want to become true, if narrative really turns into a virtual which can actualize (Shields 2013; Deleuze and Guattari 1987).

As we discussed earlier, histories of marginality, histories of distrust, of non-coordination, of short term strategies and social fragmentation can create a variety of obstacles for governance to transform itself, to understand itself, and to discern visions and paths which stand a chance (Van Assche et al. 2012). Discerning the

Real in its various manifestations is an art, as policy making is an art. It requires individual and collective judgment, cannot be reduced to rules, or to an institutional design (Miller 2002). It requires open minded discussions on past, present, future, and a clear understanding of networks and their transformations, at several scales. We noticed before that an ambition of cosmopolitanism tends to bring geo-politics into the picture. Geo-politics can be behind the creation of cosmopolitan places, by empires, while (as in Venice), communities can create empires, alter geopolitics, by creating very pragmatic forms of cosmopolitanism. Reviving cosmopolitanism can be difficult without understanding geo-political realities, and those realities can leave fewer possible versions of cosmopolitanism open for communities, either as invention or as revival.

And we know that each revival has to be an invention to a degree, in the same way that national communities and national roots are always invented, are always narrative reconstructions a posteriori, memory selections excluding alternative boundaries, excluding ideas, histories, groups and places from the story (Anderson 2006). A memory of cosmopolitanism and a trace of internal features and functioning betraying a post cosmopolitanism can help to bring back a version of cosmopolitanism, which will always be new, because of new internal and external contexts, and new semantics allowing for new understanding of those contexts (Luhmann 1995; Deleuze and Guattari 1987).

The local character of local cosmopolitanism slowly becomes clearer here. Localism does not follow immediately from a place identity, from a history or from social identities. It follows from the entanglement of these discursivities with each other and with the history of coordination in governance. Local governance does not exist in isolation, and larger narratives and higher level politics certainly play a role in cosmopolitanism at the local level, but once a community and its governance are established, it reproduces itself, based on previous governance configurations of actor/institutions and power/knowledge. What was possible in the past leaves traces in the form of stories about what was possible, of identifications with success, with perspectives on success, but also in the form of actual coordination options and tools which offer less resistance than others and which connect with certain new forms more easily than with others. As Luhmann expressed it: 'nothing better for planning than a history of planning'. Whatever comes into existence in local governance, does so after a transformation and selection. Not everything can be understood, will be allowed to enter discussion, not everything can make a difference for narrative, network and their relation. New formal institutions, produced locally or at higher levels, produce results not predictable by decision-makers, results only understandable by references to informal institutions and to what resists coordination, to the Real.

The internal ecology of governance paths, its set of co-evolutions, affects which versions of local cosmopolitanism are more likely to emerge and more likely to be sustainable (Van Assche et al. 2014a, b; Beunen et al. 2015). We started our investigations with a rough typology, and can now return to it. The relation between the parts and the whole in local cosmopolitanism can be one of privileged access to something, of privileged connectivity, or a unique mirroring of world society as

9.4 Towards a Governance Frame

it is, or of a civilization seen as leading world society (Stichweh 2000). It can be the place where the riches are accumulated, a place to find a combination of cultural, economic and intellectual resources which give the most positive impression and best possible experience of what the world has to offer. Or, it can be a place ahead of its time, offering an image of what is to come, or of what should hopefully come about in the rest of the world. It can this offer a window on the world, or on a future world, can be real and virtual. It can be active and passive, actively shaping what is to come or passively receiving the treasures of others, of other places and communities.

We can distinguish types of local cosmopolitanism according to functional domains—art, science, politics, law, economy. Venice was first an economic power house, later a place of pleasure and art, a place of cultural cosmopolitanism, repurposing old networks for new goals. And we can look at the internal complexity of a place, how this links to the outside world: the coexistence of different groups, each with networks, as in ethnic groups, or professional groups. The internal diversity can then be understood as embodying a value in itself, e.g. by spurring innovation, and it can be seen as valuable because of synergetic networks. It can be understood as a selection of distinct elements, and as a unique local blend of these elements, in terms of social identity, place identity and possibly networking.

These categories of local cosmopolitanism we consider possible, and the type emerging in a place will depend on its path of governance, in the manners described above. We add now that several things can happen at the same time. Several types can coexist, only partly dependent on the dominant narrative of cosmopolitanism. The local understanding e.g. of the links between cultural and economic networks can be different from reality, but such disjunction can exist until the actual functioning of cultural and economic networks erodes their coexistence in a given state. A locally unifying city culture of cosmopolitan patina can be invoked selectively, while internal differences can play out in other arena's. As long as these occasions and arena's are buffered, this remains possible. Narratives do not need to be entirely compatible and cohesive, for an individual and for a community, and the same holds true for narratives and networks.

9.5 Policies and Steering

What does all this mean for policies? Can we create cosmopolitan places by means of policies? We believe we said much already on this topic. First of all, that an understanding of policies as formal institutions forming and playing out in evolving governance is essential. Secondly, that reflexivity in governance, regarding the dependencies in the own governance path, the circulating narratives, the actual steering options and tools, and images of the world outside, make a difference (Luhmann 1990). One can, with the means of a centralized state, an authoritarian state, or an affluent and well-connected diasporic community, easily built a new city, bring together people, money, expertise, and create incentives for locals to establish connections outside and for outsiders to do the same inside. Or, one can think of a case like Amsterdam in the late 16th century, where various foreign groups quickly settled, took over local government, brought in their capital and connections, and turned the place into something cosmopolitan in one generation. Long histories are not always necessary.

Creating a new future is always difficult in a community, and understanding past, present, and the nature of governance and context are essential (Van Assche and Hornidge 2015; Van Assche and Verschraegen 2008). A cosmopolitan position, as we said, is a bold ambition to start with, and implies privilege, in at least one of the senses listed above. A history of cosmopolitanism makes it easier to keep it alive in some form, although maybe not in the same form. A memory of cosmopolitanism can be helpful in reinventing a new locally adapted form, but, as we saw in Sulina, it can also create obstacles for any form of sustainable governance (and, in that case, a sustainable coexistence with a fragile ecological environment).

Creating networks takes usually time however, and in most cases what we would recognize as a cosmopolitan place is endowed with networks which are not easily created quickly, and at the same time. Building a museum is not building a cultural life. Building a university is not the same as building intellectual life and spurring innovation. Forcing researchers to sit around the table with bureaucrats and entrepreneurs who tell them what innovation is and which one they expect and expect to be useful, does not lead to great innovations and to great science (which could engender more radical innovations later). Building narratives which can bind a community and inspire a cosmopolitan future is not easy and takes time. New stories about living in the best, most progressive, most cosmopolitan place in the world have effects when they are believable, first of all to the inhabitants themselves. In other words, things take time, remain unpredictable, and this is certainly true for the matching of narratives and networks, which, in a truly cosmopolitan community, is not only a matching but of synergetic coexistence. We would say that such match is a rarity, making cosmopolitanism a rarity, and providing the basic definition of local cosmopolitanism, a privilege, not the standard.

Building believable stories about being an exception is bound to be an exception, and building and recognizing the networks inspiring and being inspired by these stories is a greater endeavor even (Throgmorton 1996). Trust, ambition, leadership, reflexivity, judgment in discerning when to coordinate, to regulate, to invest are needed. Learning from other communities, their ambitions, their successes and failures, their forms of governance can help, but recipes for success do not exist. Policy transplants will have different effects in different places, and just as Silicon Valley cannot easily be replicated and summarized as a policy formula (Latour 2009; Fischer 2009), or Paris around 1900 cannot be replicated in its cosmopolitan culture by subsidizing and inviting foreign artists, the more general concept of cosmopolitanism will not bear specification in the same way everywhere. As soon as the concept and the recipe land somewhere, they will affect narratives and networks in new ways internally, and have different effects on the connectivity with other scales and communities.

9.5 Policies and Steering

Stories of slow coordination between actors, attracting new actors, trying new institutions, developing new expertise, new products, continuous reflection one's strengths and weaknesses, ones position in the world, are the most compelling to us (cf Luhmann 1995; Easterly 2014). The role of government, of universities, cultural institutions, of business, professional associations, of locals and newcomers, will have to be different in each case, but reflexivity, judgment and patience are essential. Not everything can be steered, not everything can be predicted, not every position in world society is achievable (Van Assche and Verschraegen 2008; Latour 2009). Singapore is a little miracle, but took a few generations of concerted policies, and could lean on an existing accumulation of capital, an advantageous location on shipping lanes, an existing strong port, and a population used to an authoritarian regime using a comprehensive planning approach. China offered a wealth of opportunities for foreigners, opened up selectively, and did not purposefully create cosmopolitan Shanghai, but opened a narrowly defined space where everyone was welcome, a place where economic pressures where guided to, and where quickly a cosmopolitan hub could be expected. Scarcity of access, a vast hinterland, and a strong government were key ingredients, as well as a population which was forced to abandon traditionalism during early communism.

Policy can embody and incorporate visions of the place, its past and future, its people and modes of coexistence. Governance, as the process of making policies, plans and laws, as the networks in which this takes place, is an arena for and a process of competing narratives. These include shaded or competing place narratives, cosmopolitan and otherwise. We recall the concept of the Deleuzian palimpsest, in which different narratives and identities can crystallize in and through space, and in which foreground and background, potential and actual identity can shift place at any time. Changes in affect, in intensity, in the perception of time, can cause new narratives to be foregrounded, new shades of cosmopolitanism to arise, but shifting power relations, power/knowledge configurations tied to network shifts can alter the probability of potentialities to be actualized.

Local cosmopolitanism as a narrative construct can then be understood as a discursive matrix, marked by variations and a variety of uses, that can arise more easily under certain conditions of network configuration, but that can be kept alive, remembered, transformed narratively and re-used in new discursive and network contexts. Depending on the match between network configuration and narrative matrix, the local cosmopolitanism will have different effects on political and economic networks. New versions of cosmopolitanism can enter the arena; other, more general, discourses can encourage or engender reuses or reinventions of the local cosmopolitanism; regional and broader network shifts might allow for an increased value of local narratives. The telling itself can be valuable, the place can become more attractive for people, for investment, the products can become more valuable because of a more attractive place brand.

Understanding local cosmopolitanism and its fine mechanics can open the door to a new perspective on globalization. Our perspective allows for a new articulation of the position and the possibilities of policy, in dealing with places in the margin, as well as in the center of global networks. Cosmopolitanism will be different per place, and was and is always local, because of the nature of governance, largely independent of the changing face of globalization in our times. Communities reproduce themselves through decisions, decisions informed by their understanding of themselves and the world. Each and every attempt at occupying a privileged place, will be processed in and through the configurations of governance, which will remold the stories of self and world that existed before, and built on networks and network potential which depend on larger networks, on internal linkages, and on the possibility to discern new networking potential, and new options to match networks and narratives.

References

Anderson B (2006) Imagined communities: reflections on the origin and spread of nationalism. Verso Books, London
Beunen R, Van Assche K, Duineveld M (2015) Evolutionary governance theory: theory and applications. Springer, Heidelberg
Delanty G (2009) The cosmopolitan imagination. Cambridge University Press, Cambridge
Deleuze G, Guattari A (1987) A thousand plateaus. University of Minnesota Press, Minneapolis
Easterly W (2014) The tyranny of experts: economists, dictators, and the forgotten rights of the poor. Basic Books, New York
Fischer F (1990) Technocracy and the politics of expertise. Sage, Newbury Park
Fischer F (2000) Citizens, experts, and the environment: the politics of local knowledge. Duke University Press, Durham
Fischer F (2009) Democracy and expertise: reorienting policy inquiry. Oxford University Press, Oxford
Fuchs S (2001) Against essentialism. Harvard University Press, Cambridge
Gunder M (2003) Planning policy formulation from a Lacanian perspective. Int Plann Stud 8(4):279–294
Hajer MA, Wagenaar H (eds) (2003) Deliberative policy analysis: understanding governance in the network society. Cambridge University Press, Cambridge
Jacobs J (2014) Spatial planning in cross-border regions: a systems-theoretical perspective. Plann Theor (online first)
Jacobs J, Van Assche K (2014) Understanding empirical boundaries: a systems-theoretical avenue in border studies. Geopolitics 19(1):182–205
Latour B (2009) Politics of nature. Harvard University Press, Cambridge
Luhmann N (1990) Political theory in the welfare state. Walter de Gruyter, Berlin
Luhmann N (1995) Social systems. Stanford University Press, Stanford
Mignolo W (2000) The many faces of cosmo-polis: border thinking and critical cosmopolitanism. Publ Culture 12(3):721–748
Miller HT (2002) Postmodern public policy. Suny Press, New York
Miller HT, Fox CJ (2007) Postmodern public administration. ME Sharpe, New York
Pressman JL, Wildavsky A (1984) Implementation. University of California Press, Berkeley
Roe E (1994) Narrative policy analysis: theory and practice. Duke University Press, Durham
Shields R (2013) Spatial questions: cultural topologies and social spatialisation. Sage, Thousand Oaks
Stichweh R (2000) On the genesis of world society: innovations and mechanisms. Distinktion: Scand J Soc Theor 1(1):27–38
Teubner G (1997) Global Bukowina. Legal pluralism in world society. In: Teubner G (ed) Global law without a state. Dartmouth, Brookfield, pp 3–28

Throgmorton J (1996) Planning as persuasive story telling. University of Chicago Press, Chicago
Van Assche K (2004) Signs in time. An interpretive account of urban planning and design, the people and their histories. Wageningen University, Wageningen
Van Assche K (2014a) Ernest Oberholtzer and the art of boundary crossing: writing, life and the narratives of conservation and planning. Plann Perspect 29(1):45–65
Van Assche K (2014b) Semiotics of silent lakes. Sigurd Olson and the interlacing of writing, policy and planning. J Environ Policy Plann (ahead-of-print), 1–15
Van Assche K, Verschraegen G (2008) The limits of planning: Niklas Luhmann's systems theory and the analysis of planning and planning ambitions. Plann Theory 7(3):263–283
Van Assche K, Hornidge AK (2015) Rural development. Knowledge and expertise in governance. Wageningen Academic, Wageningen
Van Assche K, Devlieger P, Teampău P, Verschraegen G (2009) Forgetting and remembering in the margins: constructing past and future in the Romanian Danube Delta. Memory Stud 2(2):211–234
Van Assche K, Duineveld M, Beunen R, Teampău P (2011a) Delineating locals. Transformations of knowledge/power and the governance of the Danube delta. J Environ Policy Plann 13(1):1–21
Van Assche K, Beunen R, Jacobs J, Teampău P (2011b) Crossing trails in the marshes. Flexibility and rigidity in the governance of the Danube delta. J Environ Plann Manage 54(8):997–1018
Van Assche K, Bell S, Teampău P (2012) Traumatic natures in the swamp. Concepts of nature and participatory governance in the Danube delta. Environ Values 21(2):163–183
Van Assche K, Shtaltovna A, Hornidge A-K (2013) Visible and invisible informalities and institutional transformation. Lessons from transition countries: Georgia, Romania, Uzbekistan. In: Hayoz N, Giordano Chr (eds) Informality and post-socialist transition. Peter Lang, Frankfurt
Van Assche K, Beunen R, Duineveld M (2014a) Evolutionary governance theory: an introduction. Springer, Heidelberg
Van Assche K, Beunen R, Duineveld M (2014b) Formal/informal dialectics and the self-transformation of spatial planning systems: an exploration. Adm Soc 46(6):654–683
van Zoest A (1978) Semiotiek. Ambo, Baarn
Whatmore S (2006) Materialist returns: practising cultural geography in and for a more-than-human world. Cult Geogr 13(4):600–609
Yanow D (2000) Conducting interpretive policy analysis. Sage, Thousand Oaks
Žižek S (2000) The ticklish subject: the absent centre of political ontology. Verso, London
Žižek S (2008) In defense of lost causes. Verso, London
Žižek S (2013) Interrogating the real. A&C Black, New York

CPSIA information can be obtained at www.ICGtesting.com
Printed in the USA
LVOW02s1653020615

440878LV00002B/12/P